Solving Business Problems

All About Spreadsheet Software

THE MICROCOMPUTER BUSINESS SOFTWARE EVALUATION SERIES

The Microcomputer Business Software Evaluation Series consists of comprehensive guides that enable microcomputer users to make informed software buying decisions.

While the series is oriented toward business software users' buying needs, the volumes are written for users at all levels of microcomputer experience. Technical terms are clearly defined and important program features are carefully examined.

Each book features timely reviews, evaluations, and comparisons of most of the major products in its software category including an in-depth look at one leading product. A unique Needs Assessment Checklist is also provided to help you thoroughly explore the many choices involved in making an intelligent buying decision.

Communicating in Writing: All About Word Processing Software

Communicating Online: All About Data Communications Software

Computerizing Your Accounting System: All About Integrated Accounting Software

Creating the Best Impression: All About Business Graphics Software

Investing for Profit: All About Investment Management Software

Managing Business Applications: All About Integrated Software

Powerhouses of Information: All About Database Management Software

Solving Business Problems: All About Spreadsheet Software

Typesetting: EPOP Graphic Arts Center
Text Design: Richard Jantz, Tulpa Productions
Production: Randy Fontes
Acquisitions Editor: Therese A. Zak
Cover Design: Jim Bernard/Peter Tyras

1	2	3	4	5	6	7	8	9	
85	86	87	88	89	90	91	92	93	YEAR

Solving Business Problems

All About Spreadsheet Software

One Point™

Hayden Book Company

A DIVISION OF HAYDEN PUBLISHING COMPANY, INC.
HASBROUCK HEIGHTS, NEW JERSEY / BERKELEY, CALIFORNIA

Acknowledgments

The research, writing, and production of this book have been a collaborative project involving the efforts of many talented people. One Point gratefully acknowledges the participation of the following writers, editors, researchers, evaluators, and consultants in the preparation of this book.

Principal writer and researcher: Stanley V. McDaniel. Chief research assistant: Sally McDaniel.

One Point Publications Staff: Stevan Cloudtree, President; Jonathan Hathaway, Executive Vice-President; Richard J. Jantz, Director & Senior Editor; Eric Knorr, Associate Editor; Trish Ventura, Assistant Editor; Cindy Fontes, Manager.

Additional editorial and technical support: Bruce Anderson, Anne Beede, Walter J. Clegg, Bill Dempsy, Kathie DeVito, Tom Evans, Rosemarie E. Falanga, Denyse Forman, Sarada Hopkins, Stephen Ritchie, John Rompel, Balfour Smith, Mike Smith, Paul Stottlemyer, Martha Strizich, and Joni Yamamoto.

Hayden Book Company Computer Science Staff: Michael Violano, Editor Director; Therese Zak, Acquisitions Editor.

Software Evaluators: Dick Andersen, Susan Baake-Kelly, Karen Beaman, Jim Bohannon, Francois Brenot, Noel Carrasco, Peggy Casey, Dan DeSalvo, Dan Ditmars, Shirley Hunt, Ann Longenecker, Kirk McClure, Brian McCue, Bill Oakes, John Propst, Mike Smith-Heimer, David Syme, and Alex Veech.

A special thanks is extended to all of the spreadsheet software publishers and distributors who made review copies of their products available for evaluation and review during the completion of this project.

Preface

An electronic spreadsheet program is a general purpose modeling tool. It does everything that an accountant's worksheet does—and quite a bit more. If your success depends even in part upon intelligent management of numbers, you can certainly benefit from using a spreadsheet program. Every manager, accountant, engineer, stockbroker, and administrator will find that spreadsheet power offers significant advantages over manual techniques.

If you're a manager considering new business activities, you can quickly calculate projected costs based on any number of variables. An electronic spreadsheet will develop just the series of models you wish—and deliver printed copies of each one for handy comparison—in a fraction of the time it would take with a calculator and a columnar pad.

Over the past several years, scores of spreadsheet programs have been written for compact, low-cost, personal computers like the IBM PC. Available to large and small businesses alike, spreadsheet software for microcomputers encourages creative management "at the desktop," contributing to reduced operating costs, increased productivity, and an enhanced sense of control over financial growth.

This book is designed to help you, as a potential software program buyer, understand the many features and functions that make up an electronic spreadsheet. It'll help you identify your specific needs, and see how those needs relate to what the market has to offer. You'll find reviews that contrast several of the most definitive spreadsheet programs available, and charts that compare these programs point by point. Armed with the information you find here, you can confidently select the program that best meets your requirements.

Although this book is aimed primarily at a business audience, it'll benefit many who are not directly involved in business, since the breadth of spreadsheet applications is practically unlimited. If you're new to computers, you'll find information on spreadsheet history, a general description of spreadsheet operations, and careful explanations of all the main spreadsheet features. More experienced readers may wish to turn directly to the product reviews and comparative charts.

This book is divided into three parts. Part I, *Electronic Spreadsheet Technology,* consists of three chapters. The first of these, *Exploring Spreadsheet Basics,* looks at common spreadsheet features and the terms used to describe them. Chapter 2, *Using an Electronic Spreadsheet,* explains special program features and discusses the differences between first- and second-generation spreadsheet programs. Chapter 3, *Charting Your Spreadsheet Needs,* explores spreadsheet features in detail and provides a Needs Assessment Checklist to help you select the best software program for your applications.

Part II, *Electronic Spreadsheet Software* is the heart of the book. Chapter 4, *Reviewing the Benchmark Products,* is an in-depth study of Multiplan and

Lotus 1-2-3, two of the most popular and powerful spreadsheet programs. A thorough understanding of the features offered by both of these products will help you develop a perspective from which you can evaluate other software.

Chapter 5, *Surveying the Competition,* provides reviews on many more spreadsheet programs currently on the market. Included are advanced versions of first-generation spreadsheets such as VisiCalc and SuperCalc2, second-generation spreadsheets like Report Manager, and the newest programs that have integrated features. Integrated software programs, like Framework, bundle graphics capabilities, data management, and word processing with spreadsheet capabilities to create multipurpose business tools.

Chapter 6, *Comparing Spreadsheet Products,* presents a series of feature-by-feature comparison tables, containing all spreadsheet programs reviewed in this book. The features listed for each program neatly correspond to the Needs Assessment Checklist in Chapter 3.

Part III, *Spreadsheet Software Resources,* includes two glossaries, one of general computer terms, and one consisting of specific spreadsheet software terms. The glossaries take special care to explain ambiguous words and concepts as well as non-standardized usage in the field. Both are cross-referenced for the less experienced user.

Program evaluations in this book have been obtained from actual business users, and are based on such criteria as ease of use, error handling, quality of documentation, and much more. The full list of criteria used by the evaluators is provided in Appendix A, *Evaluation and Review Criteria.* Appendix B, *Spreadsheet Software Directory,* lists the products reviewed in this book, as well as a thorough listing of many other available spreadsheet programs. Appendix C, *Bibliography,* lists printed reference materials in the field, including periodicals, books, and additional publications.

This book is a product of One Point, a unique distributor of microcomputer products and product information to major corporations and businesses. You may find it valuable to use the One Point™ computer information network for the most up-to-date product information available. To subscribe to this modem-accessible network, contact: One Point, 2835 Mitchell Drive, Walnut Creek, California 94598, or call (800) 222-2250.

Contents

Part III: Spreadsheet Software Resources

Solving Business Problems

All About Spreadsheet Software

Part I

Electronic Spreadsheet Technology

Chapter 1

Exploring Spreadsheet Basics

To stay competitive, every business must adapt to changing conditions and anticipate future demands. Projecting the consequences of financial decisions and planning business activities are imperative to healthy management and continuing growth. Today, an increasing number of business professionals are using electronic spreadsheets to stay on the cutting edge of financial modeling and projection.

Ever since the microcomputer entered the business environment, spreadsheet programs have been the most popular application software. Fast, hands-on resolution of business problems is the core of the spreadsheet concept. By making spreadsheet modeling simple, flexible, and accessible to all, spreadsheet programs open the door to expansion and refinement of any activity where accumulated numbers are important.

The most obvious applications of a spreadsheet program are accounting and financial modeling. But microcomputer spreadsheet software allows you to exploit modeling power for a multitude of other purposes. In fact, spreadsheets seem to generate new uses almost as fast as new users get hold of them. Here are just a few of the most common spreadsheet applications:

- Tax return preparation
- Job cost estimation
- Appointment scheduling
- IRA account assessment
- Pricing model comparison
- Insurance requirement analysis
- Personnel performance evaluation
- Cost recovery analysis
- Production scheduling
- Aging report preparation
- Invoice calculation & printout
- Scientific calculations
- Experiment analysis
- Budget preparation
- Investment projection
- Loan analysis
- Sales analysis
- Inventory control

The most far-reaching spreadsheet applications involve the *What If...?* or speculative functions. If you're considering a company-wide pay raise, for example, you also may be thinking twice about long-term effects on finances. Using its What If...? capability, a spreadsheet can allay your fears or confirm your suspicions. And if it turns out that you can't afford an across-the-board 10 percent increase, changing the raise to 7 percent will yield yet another projected result.

The electronic spreadsheet will handle these or virtually any other assumptions you present. This means you can look into the future at any financial scenario that interests you.

Before examining these more sophisticated functions, however, it's imperative to grasp basic spreadsheet concepts. This chapter takes a close look at features common to all spreadsheets and explains the terms used to describe these features. A familiar paper spreadsheet—a credit card invoice—provides the chief example, both to lay a proper groundwork and to make clear that spreadsheets, after all, have been with us for many years.

Spreadsheets Defined

If you've ever made out an income tax return, or signed a mechanic's estimate showing the potential costs for car repairs, you've seen a spreadsheet in its most basic form: figures arranged in labeled *rows* and *columns*. In fact, any itemized receipt or invoice is a type of spreadsheet. Speaking very generally, a spreadsheet may be defined as a report that organizes quantities.

Actually, there's no universal definition of "spreadsheet," and no agreed upon terminology for spreadsheet features. Therefore, one of this book's goals is to help you make your way through the tangle of spreadsheet terminology by using terms as consistently as possible. When you've learned one way of defining these terms, you'll find it easier to handle the variations that occur in different spreadsheet discussions.

The first task, then, is to establish a spreadsheet vocabulary. One way to do this is by dissecting a simple paper spreadsheet and looking at the terms used to refer to each part.

Turn to the credit card invoice shown in the upper half of Figure 1-1. As you can see, the invoice is made up of a pattern of rows and columns. The places where the rows intersect the columns are called *cells*. A cell is a rectangular area defined by the borders of a row and a column, like a two-dimensional representation of a post office box.

Spreadsheet cells are often different sizes to accommodate different kinds of items. On the invoice shown here, some of the cells are empty and some contain information. This information is called *data*.

Spreadsheet Data Types
Text data and *numeric data* are the two main kinds of information in spreadsheet cells. Text data are used primarily for labeling the columns and rows of the spreadsheet, while numeric data are used in various mathematical calculations. The lower half of Figure 1-1 sorts out the data items in the invoice according to these two data types.

Card No. *8843 856 1193 0609*		Date *6/6/85*		
Name *Jonas K. Martin*				
	Quantity	Price	Amount	
PRODUCTS AND SERVICES				
Supreme Regular (Unleaded) Diesel	*8*	*1.40*	*11*	*20*
Custom Special (10/40)	*1*	*1.50*	*1*	*50*
		Sales Tax		*10*
		TOTAL	*12*	*80*

Text Data	Numeric Data
Card #	8
8843 856 1193 0609	1.40
Date	11.20
6/6/85	1
Name	1.50
Jonas K. Martin	1.50
Quantity	.10
Price	12.80
Amount	
PRODUCTS AND SERVICES	
Supreme Regular Unleaded Diesel	
Custom Special 10/40	
Sales Tax	
TOTAL	

FIGURE 1-1 Credit Card Invoice & Data Classifications

Items of text data are usually words or phrases. But if you look closely at the list of text data in Figure 1-1, you'll see a few numbers like the date and the credit card number. Even though they are made up of digits, these numbers are not considered to be numeric data, because they are never involved in calculations. In contrast, the number 11.20 in the amount column is the result of multiplying 8 in the quantity column by 1.40 in the price column. These numbers take part in calculations and therefore count as numeric data.

The Spreadsheet Matrix

If you look at the invoice with all items of data removed, as shown in the upper half of Figure 1-2, you'll see nothing but a pattern of rows and columns. This pattern is called a spreadsheet *matrix,* which resembles an accountant's columnar pad before any entries are made.

Card No.				Date		
Name						
				Quantity	Price	Amount
PRODUCTS AND SERVICES						
Supreme	Regular	Unleaded	Diesel			
Custom	Special	10/40				
					Sales Tax	
					TOTAL	

FIGURE 1-2 Credit Card Invoice Matrix & Template

An empty matrix like the one in Figure 1-2 turns into a business form only after the rows and columns are labeled in a particular way. Certain items of text data on the list shown in Figure 1-2 do just this: They act as *labels*. A matrix is termed a *template* when it is defined by labels that allow the matrix to serve a useful purpose. The lower half of Figure 1-2 shows the invoice template—that is, the matrix with only the labels added.

Your local service station attendant usually has dozens of invoice templates like the one in Figure 1-2 stacked right beside his credit card embossing machine. They have no impact at all upon your bank account until they are filled out with *report data* (i.e., your name, credit card number, the date, and various amounts). *Entries* are the items of report data filled in by the attendant. The result is a completed invoice, or a *spreadsheet report*.

Models & Projections

A credit card invoice is a report written after the fact. You have already received the merchandise, and the invoice is merely a summary of what has happened and how much you owe. But now think about a mechanic's estimate sheet for car repairs. As you can see in Figure 1-3, it's quite different: The entries represent possible costs, rather than actual amounts paid or committed. A spreadsheet report of this kind, illustrating a possible scenario, is called a *model.*

When you shop around at different automotive repair shops for the best estimate, each estimate sheet you receive is a different spreadsheet model projecting a different scenario. For this reason spreadsheet models are also called *projections,* since they project a possible future situation.

Qty.	Part Number	Cost Ea.	Total		Labor—Description	Total	
Total Parts					Total Labor		
				Total Parts		
				Total Labor		
				Sales Tax		
				Total Amount Due		

FIGURE 1-3 Mechanic's Repair Estimate

A *financial projection* is a model of a possible financial situation, based upon deliberate variation of one or more significant report entries. These projections can answer such day-to-day questions as: "How will the budget look if we get that check from the insurance company?" or "What will be the effect on revenues if the production schedule falls five percent short of predictions?" Comparing different financial projections can give you a solid base for decision making.

Spreadsheet Organization

The value of even the simplest spreadsheet lies in the way information is gathered and presented. A good template is organized to bring out important relationships between various items of data. This often means that some data items will be repeated in different parts of the worksheet, where they will be displayed in a slightly different way.

As shown in Figure 1-3, the repair estimate has a column for "parts" and another column for "labor." The totals are entered at the bottom of each column, where they end up side by side. Since these totals will be added together, they are copied to a summary column at the bottom of the form, where they are placed one above the other. This new arrangement of the two figures makes them easy to add together, and it simplifies checking someone else's addition.

As you can see from this example, the arrangement of figures on a spreadsheet is influenced by the kind of calculations that will be performed. Calculations used in a spreadsheet report can always be expressed as mathematical formulae, but in a simple spreadsheet, formulae are usually taken for granted—that is, they are not actually printed out on the form. The person filling out the form automatically performs addition, subtraction, or multiplication as needed.

Sometimes, however, formulae needed to complete a report are written right into the form, as in this line from U.S. Federal Income Tax Form 1040:

22. Total Income. Add amounts in column for lines 7 through 21.

The expression "add amounts in column for lines 7 through 21" is a *spreadsheet formula*. If we abbreviate "Line" with L, the formula might be written like this: L7 + L8 + L9 + L10 + L11 + L12 + L13...and so on, all the way to L20 + L21 = L22.

This formula makes the value on line 22 *depend upon* the values of lines 7 through 21. Notice that the actual figures from lines 7 through 21 do not appear in the formula, since those figures will vary from taxpayer to taxpayer. Instead, the formula contains *cell references*, which means that it refers to the cells whose values will be used in the calculation.

A spreadsheet formula uses cell references in much the same way that an algebraic formula uses variables. Formulae like these are essential to the organization of the spreadsheet, so we must classify them as part of the spreadsheet's template data. Template data, then, include formulae (explicit or implicit) as well as labels.

Summarizing the Basics

This chapter has defined the terms that apply to simple paper spreadsheets. Generally speaking, a spreadsheet is a report that organizes quantities. It contains figures arranged in labeled rows and columns.

A *cell* is the area where a column and row intersect. This area is always rectangular, but its size may vary. *Data* are the information contained in cells. *Text data* are used primarily for labeling, while *numeric data* are used in mathematical calculations. Text data may include numerals used for labeling purposes.

The spreadsheet *matrix* is the bare pattern of rows and columns with the data removed. A matrix that is structured by *labels* and *formulae* is called a *template*. Formulae used in spreadsheet templates may establish mathematical relationships between specific cells of the spreadsheet by using *cell references* as variables. When a template has been filled out with *report data,* such as names, numbers, and so on, the completed product is called a *spreadsheet report.* Each item of report data is an *entry.*

Finally, a *model* is a spreadsheet report that uses data to illustrate possible situations. Models are also called *projections.* A *financial projection* is a model of a possible financial situation based upon making deliberate variations in one or more of the significant report entries. Projections are an invaluable planning and management tool.

Chapter 2

Using an Electronic Spreadsheet

Computer-enhanced spreadsheets were first limited to programs that ran on large, mainframe computers. Only companies that could afford expensive computer time could use them. There was little chance of a small business enlisting an electronic spreadsheet to plan next year's budget.

Furthermore, mainframe spreadsheet programs, often called "decision support systems," aren't designed to be operated by the layperson. Where mainframe spreadsheet programs are used, a natural separation occurs between the spreadsheet programmer, who must be a skilled technician, and the end user—typically a high-level administrator who has neither the time nor the inclination to work directly with a computer.

In 1978, this gap between computer programmer and end user was bridged by a handful of innovators. A Harvard Business School student named Dan Bricklin, and his friend, programmer Robert Frankston, developed an enhanced electronic simulation of an actual paper spreadsheet. The program projected a dynamic matrix of cells right on the display screen of a microcomputer system— that smaller and more affordable machine that has come to be called the personal or desktop computer.

Template formulae, as well as report data, could be entered directly into the cells in much the same way you would create a paper spreadsheet using a columnar pad. Dan Fylstra, also a student, founded the firm Personal Software to market the new electronic spreadsheet program, which was called VisiCalc. Since the historic arrival of VisiCalc, a great many software firms have developed electronic spreadsheets targeted for microcomputer users.

Using the terminology developed in Chapter 1, this chapter will outline the unique features that make an electronic spreadsheet more powerful and easier to use than its paper counterpart. It also focuses on many of the advanced powers and special features of second-generation spreadsheets, with an eye toward future developments in spreadsheet software.

Although this chapter is not a tutorial on spreadsheet use, it does describe many of the terms and techniques common to the majority of electronic spreadsheets. Technical terms that are presented in *italics* throughout this book are also explained in the Glossary found in Part III. Novice users who seek even more information about the operation of a microcomputer system, or about spreadsheet programs in general, are advised to consult the Bibliography (Appendix C) for additional resources.

Terms & Techniques

Any spreadsheet must begin with a matrix of cells. However, most spreadsheet programs keep the display screen from getting too crowded by omitting the grid of horizontal and vertical lines that make up a matrix. Instead, electronic spreadsheets generally create their matrices by displaying a set of row and column *coordinates* at the left side and at the top of the screen.

These coordinates are used to identify individual cells. The column coordinates are usually letters, and the row coordinates are numbers. The cells of most electronic spreadsheets are named by a letter-number combination. For example, cell A1 lies at the intersection of column A and row 1, cell B4 at the intersection of column B and row 4, and so on.

Control of the spreadsheet matrix would be much more difficult if it were not for a small but powerful helper: the spreadsheet pointer, or *cursor,* illustrated in Figure 2-1. The cursor usually appears as a bright (or blinking) rectangular box or single-character underscore that can be moved from cell to cell on the screen. When the cursor is located within a given cell (as shown in Figure 2-1), it expands or contracts to match the width of the cell.

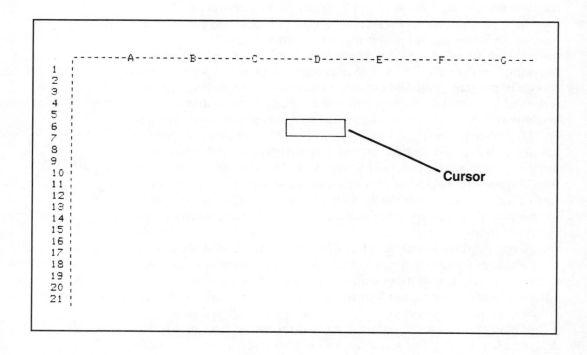

FIGURE 2-1 A Basic Spreadsheet Matrix

When you start up a spreadsheet program, all the matrix columns (and, therefore, all of the cells) have the same width. They are usually wide enough to accommodate at least nine characters. If you want to add labels longer than the initial width, the spreadsheet program must provide a command that allows you to change the width of individual columns. By using a width *formatting* command, you can tailor the shape of the spreadsheet matrix to suit your needs. For example, to accommodate a column of labels that identifies a series of spreadsheet rows, you can widen the column that holds the labels, without widening the accompanying columns of numeric data. Figure 2-2 gives an illustration of this selective cell expansion.

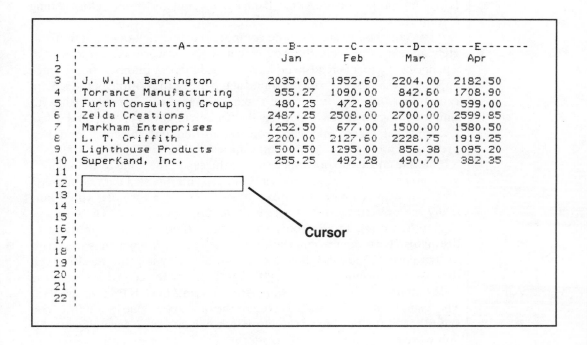

FIGURE 2-2 A Modified Spreadsheet Matrix

Most microcomputer keyboards, including that of the IBM PC, have a group of four *arrow keys* pointing up, down, right, and left. Most spreadsheet programs dedicate these keys to cursor movement. Pressing one of them will move the cursor from cell to cell in the direction of the particular arrow key pressed. For more rapid movement, various other keyboard commands allow you to make instant cursor "leaps" to distant cells.

The cell where the cursor is located is called the *active cell,* because it's the cell where you can make or change entries. To make an entry, you move the cursor to the appropriate cell, type the entry on the keyboard, and press the Enter key.

Types of Entries & Formats

When you use a printed form, such as an invoice, *entries* are simply report data that you write in preselected locations. On an electronic spreadsheet, you can develop your own labels and formulae at the computer keyboard. Since the process of typing material into a computer from the keyboard is generally called "entering" that material, spreadsheet labels and formulae, and not just report data, are referred to as *entries*.

You can't make an entry into an electronic spreadsheet unless the program is in the correct *operating mode*. Spreadsheet programs usually have at least two modes of operation: one for accepting commands, and another for accepting entries. If your program is in *command mode,* you'll have to switch it to *entry mode* before you make an entry. And if your program is in entry mode, you must switch it back to command mode before issuing a command.

As you type an entry on the computer keyboard, it does not immediately appear in the cell, the way it would if you were writing it in with a pencil on a paper spreadsheet. Instead, the letters or numbers of the entry appear on a special line, usually found at the top or the bottom of the screen, called the *edit/entry line*. If you make a mistake, you can correct it with simple editing functions (e.g., using the Backspace key to back up and delete a wrong character). Only when you are satisfied with the entry, and then press the Enter key, does the entry appear in the cell.

Some entries do not appear inside the cell in the same form in which you enter them. For example, in addition to entering text data or numeric data, you also can enter formulae. If your entry is a formula, you'll normally see only the *result* of that formula displayed in the cell.

When using an electronic spreadsheet, therefore, it's important to distinguish between the entry and the *displayed value* which is the result of that entry. Figure 2-3 illustrates a formula entry and the resulting cell display. The formula SUM(B3 to B10) is the entry for cell B12. It uses the SUM function to calculate the sum of the amounts in cells B3 through B10. The result of the addition, 10166.02, is the displayed value in cell B12. The status line at the bottom of the display shows the actual formula entry. If you were to move the cursor to another cell, a different entry would appear on the status line.

In more advanced spreadsheets, the displayed value in a given cell may be formatted by issuing an appropriate command. For example, a cell may be given *dollars-and-cents format.* If you enter the number 10 and the cell has been given the dollars-and-cents format, the cell will not display the number 10, but instead will show $10.00.

Comma format will place a comma before every three digits, so that an entry of 1000 will be displayed as 1,000. *Fixed decimal format* will display a numeric entry up to a fixed number of decimal places, and so on. Formatting commands save time, provide flexibility, and give your report a clearer, more readable appearance.

The Dynamic Template

The ability to enter formulae and have their results displayed in cells is enhanced by a feature that allows cell references to be used as variables in the formulae. In Figure 2-3, the formula SUM(B3 to B10) uses cell

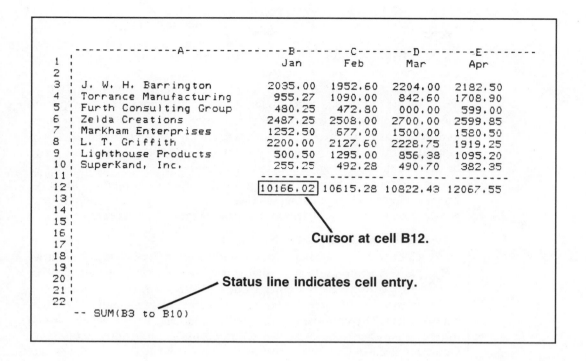

```
                - - - - - - - - - - - - - A - - - - - - - - - - - - - - B - - - - - - - - C - - - - - - - - - D - - - - - - - - E - - - - - - - -
    1 ¦                                                           Jan       Feb       Mar       Apr
    2 ¦
    3 ¦ J. W. H. Barrington                                  2035.00   1952.60   2204.00   2182.50
    4 ¦ Torrance Manufacturing                                955.27   1090.00    842.60   1708.90
    5 ¦ Furth Consulting Group                                480.25    472.80    000.00    599.00
    6 ¦ Zelda Creations                                      2487.25   2508.00   2700.00   2599.85
    7 ¦ Markham Enterprises                                  1252.50    677.00   1500.00   1580.50
    8 ¦ L. T. Griffith                                       2200.00   2127.60   2228.75   1919.25
    9 ¦ Lighthouse Products                                   500.50   1295.00    856.38   1095.20
   10 ¦ SuperKand, Inc.                                       255.25    492.28    490.70    382.35
   11 ¦                                                     ---------  --------  --------  --------
   12 ¦                                                    |10166.02| 10615.28 10822.43 12067.55
   13 ¦
   14 ¦
   15 ¦
   16 ¦                                              Cursor at cell B12.
   17 ¦
   18 ¦
   19 ¦
   20 ¦                                      Status line indicates cell entry.
   21 ¦
   22 ¦
        -- SUM(B3 to B10)
```

FIGURE 2-3 Displayed Value

references to call for the sum of the values in cells B3 through B10. The formula is treated *dynamically* by the program—if the values in the referenced cells change, the displayed value in cell A5 also will change.

Using powerful calculating and editing features like these, you can construct dynamic spreadsheet templates with a web of active mathematical relations among the cells. The process of modeling comes to life because the spreadsheet program can recalculate all of the displayed values almost immediately after you make changes in numeric data or in formulae.

Any time you wish, you can save a particular model or report on a floppy disk, or print it out in hardcopy. By loading the saved report from the disk and back into the computer's memory, and then entering new values, your report acts as a template. If you lack the mathematical know-how needed to produce a particular template, you can purchase ready-made templates either on disk, or in book form which you can enter yourself.

Windows & Split Screens

Electronic spreadsheets come in many different sizes. A standard size for early spreadsheet programs was about 255 rows by 64 columns, but there are electronic spreadsheets as small as 30 rows by 20 columns, and others that number rows and columns in the thousands.

Since the average computer screen is 24 lines long by 80 characters wide, the screen displays only a portion of the entire spreadsheet at any given time. You may bring other portions into view as needed by using *scrolling* commands entered at the keyboard. Because the screen only shows part of the spreadsheet at a time, it's often called a *window*. Scrolling commands "move" this window across the spreadsheet, framing the various areas you want to appear onscreen.

Some spreadsheet programs allow you to split the screen into two or more smaller windows, each of which shows a different part of the spreadsheet. The split screen feature makes it possible to create different reports in different areas of the spreadsheet, and then view them simultaneously as a single image. For example, you can set up reports for four different quarters of the year in different areas of the spreadsheet, and then split the screen into four windows and scroll through all the quarters simultaneously. The scrolling may be linked, which is called *synchronous scrolling,* or each window may be scrolled separately, called *asynchronous scrolling*.

Spreadsheet Command Structure

Every electronic spreadsheet comes with a set of commands—such as Delete, Move, Print, and Save—that is used to control the program. The basic set of commands is similar from one spreadsheet to another, but some spreadsheet programs offer a richer group of commands than their counterparts. The commands are usually organized into a treelike structure of groups and subgroups. *Primary commands* are those that are immediately accessible when you start up the spreadsheet program, while *secondary commands* become available only after you execute a particular primary command.

If your spreadsheet program is designed to start up in entry mode, the primary commands will include basic text entry and editing commands, as well as a command to switch into command mode—typically by pressing the slash (/) key. As soon as the slash key is pressed, the secondary commands become available. Most of these secondary commands will, in their turn, make a subgroup of command options accessible.

As a result of this "treelike" structure, spreadsheet commands usually require you to execute a brief sequence of keystrokes in order to reach the desired command level. To print out a spreadsheet, for example, you might enter the command "/O" for output. This would bring you to another level of commands, from which you would select "P" for printer, followed by the appropriate filename.

Typing these sequences soon becomes second nature, but for beginners, a good spreadsheet program will display the command options available at each stage of command entry. The options are shown on the *command line,* which appears at the top or the bottom of the screen.

Since you issue commands and data entries at different times, the same onscreen location may act as both the command line and the edit/entry line. Figure 2-4 provides an example of the second level of storage command options used by InteCalc (from Schuchardt Software Systems, Inc.). From this point in the command chain, reached by entering "/S," typing any of the option letters will move the program to the option selected. For example, pressing "D" will activate file deletion procedures. The file delete keystroke sequence, then, is "/SD." Note that the line also serves as a *status line,* showing (at the far right) the current cursor location, the current column width, and the percentage of usable memory remaining.

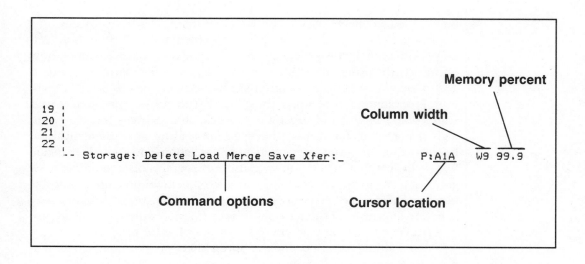

FIGURE 2-4 InteCalc Command Line

If you make a mistake part way down a command tree, most spreadsheet programs provide a way for you to "back up" to the previous level, or to move all the way back to the first level and start over again. The Escape key is commonly used for one or both of these purposes. Good spreadsheet software should also offer online help information, in the event of error, or instructions to remind you how to use program functions. As you'll see in the following section, newer programs give a great deal more attention to the needs of the user who is not technically oriented.

Advanced Programs & Features

Following the debut of VisiCalc, a number of similar spreadsheet programs were introduced. These programs, including VisiCalc, became known as "first-generation" spreadsheets. Among the members of this group are VisiCalc, SuperCalc, PeachCalc, and CalcStar. First-generation programs were designed to run on computers with a relatively small amount of internal memory (64 kilobytes or less), and therefore were limited in overall program capability.

The limitations of these early programs are particularly evident when you consider the average size of a first-generation spreadsheet's matrix— typically 254 rows by 64 columns. (CalcStar exceeded this somewhat with a grid of 255 rows by 127 columns). These sizes may seem large in comparison to an accountant's ledger sheet, but an electronic spreadsheet can lend itself to a different use of space than a paper version, partly because of its flexibility.

For one thing, it's handy to connect related reports mathematically, but this usually can't be done unless the reports exist within the same matrix. The result is that a single matrix begins to take on the burden of a whole book of ledger sheets. When you've set up many smaller templates on a single 254 by 64 matrix, you may have trouble finding them without getting disoriented. Finding the template you want depends partly upon how effectively the program can scroll from one part of the matrix to another, and in many first-generation spreadsheets, scrolling methods are limited.

Programmers were quick to realize that electronic spreadsheet software could benefit from larger and more flexible matrices, a correspondingly richer set of commands, and expansion of available mathematical and logical operations. In addition to memory restrictions and limited command features, most first-generation spreadsheet programs offered only a basic group of mathematical operations. Very few of them featured programmable functions, and some even lacked trigonometrical functions. A natural way of expressing quantity comparisons, via bar charts or other kinds of graphs, was either not provided or offered only in crude form.

Even a little experience with a spreadsheet program will reveal that it can be a valuable data resource—spreadsheets have a habit of collecting labeled lists of numbers and text. Yet first-generation spreadsheets are generally short on text-editing and data-handling commands. Most of them could copy or move blocks of data with a simple command, but such useful features as list sorting, global search and replace, or the ability to exchange information easily with other programs, were generally missing.

Fortunately, this situation didn't last long. By mid-1982, major software firms were introducing more sophisticated and powerful spreadsheet software. These programs took advantage of current technology, including the increased memory capacity and speed of new 16-bit personal computers such as the IBM PC. Because of their association with a new breed of computer, as well as their expanded capacities, the newer programs have come to be known as "second-generation" spreadsheets.

The differences between first- and second-generation spreadsheet packages, however, are not uniform. Generally speaking, a spreadsheet program must satisfy the following four conditions to be classified as a member of the second generation:

- It must be long on memory.
- It must allow linkage between two or more separately stored models.
- It must include expanded calculating and formatting capabilities.
- It must offer online help.

Second-generation spreadsheets generally require more memory to operate, but memory utilization is superior, resulting in increased speed and efficiency. Some second-generation spreadsheet programs include a *virtual memory* feature that allows use of disk storage space to increase the amount of memory available for building a spreadsheet report.

Matrix sizes of 999 rows by 99 columns are common among second-generation programs. This rises dramatically in the case of three-dimensional spreadsheets, which may have matrices comprised of over 16 million possible cells. At these levels, electronic spreadsheet programs approach the capabilities of mainframe-style financial modeling languages.

Of course, the size of the report you can actually build with such massive programs depends upon your hardware and its available storage. The chief advantage of extremely large matrices is the flexibility of arrangement they may provide. The situation is somewhat analogous to high wattage in a stereo amplifier. You don't actually crank up the full 100 watts of power available, but the extra watts provide a "buffer" in case of overload, keeping your sound clean even at high volumes.

In addition to better memory utilization and larger matrices, second-generation spreadsheets usually offer a way to "link" reports. *Sheet-linking* allows formulae and functions in one report to reference data in another. For example, regional reports may be linked to an overall company report so that a change in any regional data will update that of the company. Many newer programs also offer *consolidation,* which permits overlaying of separate reports to create a single combined report.

Finally, one of the most valuable improvements of all is the richer set of *built-in functions* that greatly simplifies template formulae. You can find trigonometrical and mathematical functions, such as Sine, Cosine, Sum, and Integer, as well as statistical functions like Count, Average, Maximum, Minimum, and Standard Deviation. Financial functions may include Net Present Value, Future Value, payment, and annuity. Logical functions such as "if...then...else," "and," "or," and "not" are also fairly common. Some second-generation programs even have functions that perform date and time arithmetic.

Help When You Need It

Error prevention and recovery is an important aspect of spreadsheet programming. Beyond the ability to back out of an unwanted situation, other assistance should be available in the form of *error messages* and *help screens.* Unfortunately, some of the first spreadsheet programs tended to give vague error messages, like "Error" or (worse yet) "Fatal Error," and their help screens were frustratingly limited to obscure command summaries.

Second-generation spreadsheets generally offer a much better array of help procedures than those of the first generation, making them easier to learn and use. When you make an incorrect entry, a message usually appears indicating the nature of an error and what you should do to correct it. Your correction options are called *error recovery procedures,* and a crucial item of error recovery is the ability to prevent extreme or fatal errors that may result in the loss of a spreadsheet report. The better programs make it next to impossible to commit a fatal error.

Of course, the best way to recover from an error is not to make it in the first place, so many second-generation spreadsheets provide a constant flow of help throughout the command process. The options listed on the command line are likely to be expressed in understandable English words. In some cases, you can use English words to name cells for cell references in formulae, so that your formula entries become less prone to error.

In contrast with first-generation spreadsheets, which had help screens that were usually nothing more than a list of commands, second-generation help screens are likely to give more detailed explanations, sometimes amounting to onscreen mini-tutorials. The trend is toward *context-sensitive* help screens—that is, the screen you need most is the one you get. A touch of the help key (usually designated as the F1 function key on the IBM PC) switches the screen display from the spreadsheet matrix to the appropriate help screen.

The Trend Toward Integration

At first, the new generation of spreadsheet software seemed content with expansion and refinement of features which, in the long run, still focused on standard spreadsheet modeling. But more recently, programs have been introduced that allow you to combine financial information with other kinds of data. These products are called "integrated" spreadsheet programs, because they typically combine graphics, word processing, and database management capacities in a single package with a spreadsheet foundation.

The development toward integrated spreadsheet programs is well illustrated by SuperCalc (from Sorcim/IUS). SuperCalc, a first-generation program, was introduced in 1980 with features similar to those of VisiCalc. In 1983, SuperCalc2 was released as a second-generation spreadsheet program having upgraded memory utilization, a matrix of 9999 by 127 (compared to the original's 254 by 63), sheet consolidation, a more efficient order of calculation, and simple data management functions. SuperCalc3, following closely after SuperCalc2, added graphics, greater speed, a larger matrix, additional financial functions, and sophisticated database management—therefore qualifying it to be counted among integrated, second-generation spreadsheets.

Summing Up the Electronic Spreadsheet

This chapter has outlined the general characteristics common to most electronic spreadsheets and described the unique enhancements offered by second-generation spreadsheet software.

The matrix of an electronic spreadsheet is defined by a set of row and column *coordinates* that appears at the left side and at the top of the display screen. Column coordinates are usually letters, and row coordinates are numbers. Most spreadsheets let you vary the width of individual columns as needed.

The cursor acts as a cell pointer that you move from cell to cell using the arrow keys or other keyboard commands. The cursor width always matches the cell width, and the cell at the location of the cursor is called the *active cell*. Entries are typed in from the keyboard, and entered into the active cell with the Enter key.

Spreadsheets usually have two modes of operation: *command mode* and *entry mode*. Labels, formulae, and numeric data are all classified as entries. Typed entries first appear on the *edit/entry line* of the screen. If the entry is a formula, only the *result* of the formula, called the *displayed value*, is normally shown in the cell.

Cell references (A1, D14, etc.) may be used as variables in formulae. Their value is determined by the value currently displayed in the cells they name. Using formulae containing cell references, spreadsheet cells are linked mathematically to form a *dynamic* template. Changes made in values at one point in a report cause *recalculation* of all linked values.

Some advanced spreadsheets support *cell formatting* options, including *dollars-and-cents format, integer format, comma format,* and *fixed decimal format.* When you enter a number into a cell having a particular format setting, the displayed value in the cell will take on the specified format.

The *command line* is a line on the display screen that shows current command options. Spreadsheet commands are usually organized in a treelike structure of groups and subgroups. If you make a mistake while moving down the command tree, error recovery procedures usually will allow you to cancel the command and try again.

First-generation spreadsheet software was designed for computers with 64 kilobytes (or less) of internal memory, and were limited in overall program capability. Second-generation spreadsheet software is more powerful than the earlier group of programs. To qualify as a second-generation spreadsheet, a program must have a larger memory capacity, allow linkage between reports, and offer expanded calculating, formatting, and online help functions. "Integrated" spreadsheets combine such applications as graphics, word processing, and database management all in a single package.

Chapter 3

Charting Your Spreadsheet Needs

◆ A spreadsheet program is a complex interweaving of commands, operations, display characteristics, and results. Besides large matrices and a wealth of financial, statistical, and logical functions, many microcomputer spreadsheet programs come packaged with additional applications such as business graphics, database management, and word processing. Sorting through these many incarnations to find the best possible program for your own business needs can be a formidable task.

Before you begin selecting a program, you should have a clear idea of your requirements. This chapter is designed to help you determine exactly what you're looking for in a spreadsheet program, and to help you match your needs to what the market has to offer. A Needs Assessment Checklist provides the vehicle for this evaluation process.

The Checklist is divided into two sections: a General Checklist and a Product Comparison Checklist. The General Checklist asks basic questions about your intended applications, helping you to conceptualize how a spreadsheet will function in your working environment. It covers such issues as the number and skills level of spreadsheet users, and the investment necessary to get your system up and running. If you're in the process of buying a computer system, you'll be able to consider your software requirements as a major factor in hardware buying decisions.

The Product Comparison Checklist is organized into sections that correspond to the product comparison charts in Chapter 6. This part of the worksheet enables you to compare three programs at once, feature by feature, so you'll be able to see at a glance which program offers you the best set of options. The explanations of these features later in this chapter should further clarify the spreadsheet technology discussed in earlier chapters.

To begin, first fill in the General Checklist. Then proceed to Part II of this book. After a close read of the software reviews in Chapters 4 and 5, and the product comparison tables in Chapter 6, select the three spreadsheet products most attractive to you, and return to this chapter to use the remainder of the Checklist to thoroughly compare them.

Filling out the Checklist will take you through the many available spreadsheet features, and provide you with an invaluable evaluation tool. (The actual test instrument used for evaluating the spreadsheet software in this book is located in Appendix A).

GENERAL CHECKLIST

APPLICATIONS

1. Primary reason(s) for purchasing a spreadsheet program:
   Financial modeling   _____
   Statistical analysis   _____
   Accounting   _____
   Scientific calculations   _____
   Other: _____
   _____

2. System Users:
   Number of users   _____
   Level of user experience (use percentage):
   Beginner   _____   Advanced   _____
   Intermediate   _____   Expert   _____
   Number of users who will require training   _____
   Training by: In-house user _____   Outside consultant   _____

HARDWARE

3. Microcomputer _____

4. Operating system(s) _____

5. Total system memory (RAM)   _____ K

6. Disk storage: Number of floppy disk drives   _____
   Capacity of each floppy disk drive   _____ K
   Total floppy capacity   _____ K
   Capacity of hard disk   _____ K
   Total system capacity   _____ K

7. Printer _____

8. Graphics card _____

BUDGET & PROGRAM SELECTION

9. Budget

	Software	Hardware
Initial purchase	$ _____	$ _____
Add-on software/hardware	$ _____	$ _____
Training aids/consultants	$ _____	$ _____
Total budget	$ _____	$ _____

10. List of spreadsheet programs in this book that meet your basic requirements, and that are compatible with your computer and operating system(s).

1. _____   5. _____

2. _____   6. _____

3. _____   7. _____

4. _____   8. _____

11. From the previous list, select three programs you want to compare in depth and use the numbers you assign them throughout the remainder of this worksheet.

	Product Name	Publisher	Price
1.	_____	_____	$ _____
2.	_____	_____	$ _____
3.	_____	_____	$ _____

PRODUCT COMPARISON CHECKLIST

BASIC INFORMATION

1. General considerations:
   - Operating system   1. _____ 2. _____ 3. _____
   - Language program written in   1. _____ 2. _____ 3. _____
   - Minimum memory (RAM) required   1. _____ 2. _____ 3. _____
   - Virtual memory capability   1. ☐ 2. ☐ 3. ☐
   - Hard disk compatible   1. ☐ 2. ☐ 3. ☐
   - Copy protected   1. ☐ 2. ☐ 3. ☐
   - Demo disk   1. ☐ 2. ☐ 3. ☐

2. Product support:
   - Vendor phone support   1. _____ 2. _____ 3. _____
   - Defective disk replacement   1. _____ 2. _____ 3. _____

DOCUMENTATION

1. Manual: Index   1. ☐ 2. ☐ 3. ☐
   - Tutorial   1. ☐ 2. ☐ 3. ☐
   - Glossary of error messages   1. ☐ 2. ☐ 3. ☐
   - Glossary of terms   1. ☐ 2. ☐ 3. ☐

2. Other aids: Tutorial on disk   1. ☐ 2. ☐ 3. ☐
   - Sample files on disk   1. ☐ 2. ☐ 3. ☐
   - Quick reference card   1. ☐ 2. ☐ 3. ☐
   - Keyboard templates   1. ☐ 2. ☐ 3. ☐

3. Online help: Available any time   1. ☐ 2. ☐ 3. ☐
   - Context sensitive   1. ☐ 2. ☐ 3. ☐

SCREEN CHARACTERISTICS

1. Number of: Rows   1. _____   2. _____   3. _____
                Columns   1. _____   2. _____   3. _____
                Windows   1. _____   2. _____   3. _____

2. Jump to chosen cell   1. ☐   2. ☐   3. ☐
      Title locking   1. ☐   2. ☐   3. ☐
      Title spillover   1. ☐   2. ☐   3. ☐

3. Scrolling: Synchronous   1. ☐   2. ☐   3. ☐
                Asynchronous   1. ☐   2. ☐   3. ☐

4. Page dimension (3D)   1. ☐   2. ☐   3. ☐

5. Screen displays: Memory status   1. ☐   2. ☐   3. ☐
                     Current filename   1. ☐   2. ☐   3. ☐
                     Caps Lock indicator   1. ☐   2. ☐   3. ☐
                     Num Lock indicator   1. ☐   2. ☐   3. ☐
                     Color highlighting   1. ☐   2. ☐   3. ☐
                     Hides coordinates   1. ☐   2. ☐   3. ☐

6. Data entry aids: User prompt messages   1. ☐   2. ☐   3. ☐
                     Forms mode   1. ☐   2. ☐   3. ☐

EDITING FUNCTIONS

1. Edit cell contents   1. ☐   2. ☐   3. ☐
      Set cursor direction   1. ☐   2. ☐   3. ☐

2. Erase range of cells   1. ☐   2. ☐   3. ☐
      Move/copy range of cells   1. ☐   2. ☐   3. ☐
      Replicate function   1. ☐   2. ☐   3. ☐
      Copy cell format   1. ☐   2. ☐   3. ☐

3. Delete column/row   1. ☐   2. ☐   3. ☐
      Insert column/row   1. ☐   2. ☐   3. ☐
      Clear report   1. ☐   2. ☐   3. ☐

4. Tab search function   1. ☐   2. ☐   3. ☐
      Global search and replace   1. ☐   2. ☐   3. ☐

5. English cell names   1. ☐   2. ☐   3. ☐
      English range names   1. ☐   2. ☐   3. ☐

CELL FORMATTING

1. Automatic commas   1. ☐   2. ☐   3. ☐
      Dollars and cents   1. ☐   2. ☐   3. ☐
      Credit/debit notation   1. ☐   2. ☐   3. ☐
      Parentheses for negative   1. ☐   2. ☐   3. ☐
      Aligns numbers by decimal point   1. ☐   2. ☐   3. ☐

2. Mixed cells   1. ☐ 2. ☐ 3. ☐
   Cell protection   1. ☐ 2. ☐ 3. ☐

3. Text justification: Right   1. ☐ 2. ☐ 3. ☐
                     Left   1. ☐ 2. ☐ 3. ☐
                     Center   1. ☐ 2. ☐ 3. ☐

4. Number justification: Right   1. ☐ 2. ☐ 3. ☐
                     Left   1. ☐ 2. ☐ 3. ☐
                     Center   1. ☐ 2. ☐ 3. ☐

5. Center titles: Horizontally 1. ☐ 2. ☐ 3. ☐
                 Vertically   1. ☐ 2. ☐ 3. ☐

6. Adjust column width: Individually 1. ☐ 2. ☐ 3. ☐
                     Globally   1. ☐ 2. ☐ 3. ☐

7. Graphics format   1. ☐ 2. ☐ 3. ☐
   Adjust row height   1. ☐ 2. ☐ 3. ☐
   Display formulae in cells 1. ☐ 2. ☐ 3. ☐
   Hide cell contents   1. ☐ 2. ☐ 3. ☐

8. Percent format for decimals 1. ☐ 2. ☐ 3. ☐
   Scientific notation   1. ☐ 2. ☐ 3. ☐
   Two decimal   1. ☐ 2. ☐ 3. ☐
   Fixed decimal   1. ☐ 2. ☐ 3. ☐
   Integer format   1. ☐ 2. ☐ 3. ☐
   Global formatting options 1. ☐ 2. ☐ 3. ☐

PRINT FORMATTING

1. Printer installation program 1. ☐ 2. ☐ 3. ☐
   Printer setup strings   1. ☐ 2. ☐ 3. ☐

2. Select control codes   1. ☐ 2. ☐ 3. ☐
   Graphics output   1. ☐ 2. ☐ 3. ☐
   Use alternate font   1. ☐ 2. ☐ 3. ☐
   Print formulae   1. ☐ 2. ☐ 3. ☐
   Print screen contents   1. ☐ 2. ☐ 3. ☐

3. Print partial report   1. ☐ 2. ☐ 3. ☐
   Print report in pages   1. ☐ 2. ☐ 3. ☐
   Fit output to paper   1. ☐ 2. ☐ 3. ☐
   Report generator   1. ☐ 2. ☐ 3. ☐

FILE HANDLING

1. Specify logged drive   1. ☐ 2. ☐ 3. ☐

2. Read partial report   1. ☐ 2. ☐ 3. ☐
   Save partial report   1. ☐ 2. ☐ 3. ☐
   Copy file command   1. ☐ 2. ☐ 3. ☐

	1.	2.	3.
Delete file command	☐	☐	☐
Rename file command	☐	☐	☐
3. Reads: ASCII files	☐	☐	☐
DIF files	☐	☐	☐
SDI files	☐	☐	☐
SYLK files	☐	☐	☐
4. Merge files command	☐	☐	☐
Consolidate report	☐	☐	☐
Link individual cells	☐	☐	☐
Link separate reports	☐	☐	☐

RECALCULATION

	1.	2.	3.
1. Manual option	☐	☐	☐
Recalculate by column	☐	☐	☐
Recalculate by row	☐	☐	☐
2. Natural recalculation	☐	☐	☐
Recalculate upon loading	☐	☐	☐

MATHEMATICAL & TRIGONOMETRIC FUNCTIONS

	1.	2.	3.
1. Raise to a power	☐	☐	☐
Square root	☐	☐	☐
Sign of value	☐	☐	☐
Modulo	☐	☐	☐
2. Logarithm	☐	☐	☐
Tangent	☐	☐	☐
Cosine	☐	☐	☐
Sine	☐	☐	☐
Arc tangent	☐	☐	☐
Arc cosine	☐	☐	☐
Arc sine	☐	☐	☐
Radian/degree conversion	☐	☐	☐
Pi	☐	☐	☐
3. Sum of a list	☐	☐	☐
Integer value	☐	☐	☐
Rounded value	☐	☐	☐
Absolute value	☐	☐	☐
Random value	☐	☐	☐

FINANCIAL & STATISTICAL FUNCTIONS

	1.	2.	3.
1. Future value	☐	☐	☐
Net present value	☐	☐	☐
Internal rate of return	☐	☐	☐
Payment	☐	☐	☐

	1.	2.	3.
Depreciation	☐	☐	☐
Annuity	☐	☐	☐
Interest on loan	☐	☐	☐
2. Average value in list	☐	☐	☐
Maximum value in list	☐	☐	☐
Minimum value in list	☐	☐	☐
Count items in list	☐	☐	☐
Modal value	☐	☐	☐
3. Sum of squares	☐	☐	☐
Standard deviation	☐	☐	☐
Regression analysis	☐	☐	☐
Variance	☐	☐	☐

Other: _____

LOGICAL & SPECIALIZED FUNCTIONS

	1.	2.	3.
1. Alphabetic sorting	☐	☐	☐
Numeric sorting	☐	☐	☐
Choose	☐	☐	☐
Lookup	☐	☐	☐
2. Logical operators: And	☐	☐	☐
Or	☐	☐	☐
Not	☐	☐	☐
Nested conditionals	☐	☐	☐
If…then	☐	☐	☐
If…then…else	☐	☐	☐
3. Date entries	☐	☐	☐
Time entries	☐	☐	☐
4. Displays: Today's date	☐	☐	☐
Time of day	☐	☐	☐
Day of week	☐	☐	☐
5. Calculates: Date intervals	☐	☐	☐
Time intervals	☐	☐	☐

INTEGRATED FUNCTIONS

	1.	2.	3.
1. Built-in graphics	☐	☐	☐
2. Built-in word processing	☐	☐	☐
3. Built-in database management	☐	☐	☐
4. Built-in data communications	☐	☐	☐
5. Keystroke macros	☐	☐	☐
6. Internal programming language	☐	☐	☐

The remainder of this chapter discusses each numbered item on the Checklist. If you read these explanations with your own spreadsheet needs in mind, you can determine which program features are the most useful, and which are only marginally relevant to your applications.

The primary goal of this chapter is to help you find a spreadsheet that will provide you with the reports you require. For that, you need the right set of program features. Even if you think you've found a program with the ideal features and functions, it's a good idea to see your dealer and give it a thorough hands-on test.

General Checklist

This part of the Checklist allows you to create a profile of your most basic user requirements. Keep in mind that these needs may expand considerably in the future. In the case of hardware, most experienced users agree that it's better to purchase a minimal version of a powerful computer system than a full-blown version of a limited system. Then, as your needs grow, you'll be able to upgrade your current system, rather than find yourself shopping for a new one.

1. From the broad categories listed here, choose your most likely applications for an electronic spreadsheet. Other uses that come to mind also should be listed in the space provided. Rank all your anticipated applications in order of their importance, and refer to them as you compare spreadsheet products.

2. The expertise of prospective users in your business environment may affect your selection of software. If several users will be working with a single spreadsheet program, make certain their skills level is commensurate with the program you select.

Most programs cater to beginning users by providing onscreen lists of command options called *menus*. Menus are helpful for beginners because they route them to the commands needed to perform specific operations. The best spreadsheets also accommodate advanced users by allowing them to bypass menus once they understand program functions.

Documentation, discussed below, is another important factor. If the manual that accompanies your software is on the cryptic side, keep in mind that a number of popular programs with poorly written manuals have engendered entire books that attempt to fill the learning gap. Sometimes, online help can make up for what the manual lacks.

Even if the program you select is extremely "friendly" to the beginner, you may wish to hold formal training sessions for your personnel. Well-run instruction can save you valuable startup time and ease the anxiety of personnel unfamiliar with computers.

3. This book assumes you'll be using an IBM PC or a computer that is IBM-compatible. However, many of the programs reviewed in this book are available in versions that will run on other types of computers.

4. The operating system is the software that orchestrates the basic functions of your computer system. PC-DOS, which is IBM's version of MS-DOS, has become the operating system that most resembles an industry standard. Other common operating systems are CP/M and CP/M-86.

5. Total system memory refers to the maximum capacity of your computer's *random access memory* (RAM). This is the "workspace" of your computer, where your software and data interact. A standard IBM PC comes with 256K of RAM, enough to accommodate most second-generation spreadsheet programs.

However, some spreadsheets require more memory, and for that you need to purchase memory expansion boards, designed to plug into slots already built into your computer's chassis. Check with your computer dealer to find the type of memory boards you will need to expand your memory to the necessary capacity.

6. *Disk drives* are the most common external memory devices employed by microcomputers. Disk drives commonly use 5 1/4-inch *floppy disks,* which contain a flexible electromagnetic medium that holds data and program information.

Generally, the maximum memory capacity for a 5 1/4-inch disk drive is 320K. As you use spreadsheet software, you'll find that only a fixed number of spreadsheet reports will fit on a single disk. By the same token, some large programs are written on several floppy disks, requiring you to "swap" disks to perform different program functions.

Some computers (such as the IBM PC-XT and PC-AT) contain *hard disks,* which have many times the memory capacity of floppy disk drives. A hard disk can hold even the largest spreadsheet program in its entirety, making disk swapping unnecessary. Hard disks are also faster, more reliable, and more expensive than floppy disk drives.

7. Printers come in many sizes, run at different speeds, and print in different type styles and column widths. There are two basic types of printers: *dot matrix* and *letter quality.* The dot matrix printer is faster and cheaper than its letter quality counterpart. It also can print graphics—a must for those who wish to use spreadsheets in conjunction with a graphics application. While letter quality printers lack graphics capability, they produce output that looks professionally typed, making them ideal for producing formal reports.

8. Some spreadsheets (or almost any software containing a graphics application) require a graphics card, giving you the ability to create graphic output. This card slips into a slot inside your computer in much the same manner as the plug-in memory board described above.

9. Fill in the price you expect to pay up front for both software and hardware. You may wish to add to your initial purchase of software by buying add-on programs designed to assist in template construction, which are available from most spreadsheet software publishers. Or, you may want to get a compatible graphics application, in which case you'll probably need an additional piece of hardware—a graphics card.

Most basic spreadsheet functions are easy to learn. However, the more advanced functions—particularly those involving logical operators and financial or statistical functions—may require additional training aids. These may take the form of books, outside classes, or cassette-based training packages. Hiring a consultant is the most expensive alternative, but one that may expedite the learning process significantly by providing information tailored to your work environment.

10. All programs in this book are listed on the Contents page. After reading Chapters 1 and 2, and after surveying the products reviewed in Chapters 4 and 5, you should have an idea of your spreadsheet software needs. Based on what you've read about the software products in this book, fill in the blanks with the programs you feel could suit your needs.

11. From the preceeding list, choose three programs you feel come closest to the ideal spreadsheet program for your purposes. Product publishers and addresses can be found in Appendix B, Spreadsheet Software Directory, and prices are listed in Chapter 6, Table 6-1. The numbers (1, 2, 3) you assign these products correspond to the three numbered columns that appear throughout the Product Comparison Checklist. Using the provided format, you can compare spreadsheet "finalists" by checking off features point by point.

Product Comparision Checklist

This part of the Checklist will help you determine which of the products reviewed in this book comes closest to matching your own requirements. Used in conjunction with the product comparison charts in Chapter 6, the Checklist will allow you to thoroughly compare program features.

1. Many of the programs reviewed in this book are compatible with more than one operating system. Make a note of the operating system you intend to use (e.g., PC-DOS or CP/M 86).

Languages used for writing spreadsheet programs include assembly language (closest to the actual machine language of the computer), the "C" programming language, Pascal, Forth, and BASIC. Although other design features enter in, as a general rule a program written in assembly language is much faster than one written in BASIC.

The minimum amount of memory required for the software you purchase is a rough estimate, since it depends on the size and complexity of the spreadsheet reports you construct. If you expect to make frequent use of specialized mathematical calculations, you may find that your spreadsheet is taking more than the minimum memory listed for the program. As a general guide, a report of moderate mathematical complexity will take up about 14K of RAM by the time you reach 1,000 cells.

Very large reports are made possible by utilizing "virtual memory," a technique of accessing disk space when internal memory is exhausted. Some spreadsheet programs locate only a single command at a time in RAM, swapping commands from the disk each time a new one is requested. But swapping techniques that frequently access the disk for extra memory can slow down program operation significantly.

A sensible approach to the memory problem is to select a program that allots a sizable amount of RAM for your reports, using virtual memory only when it becomes necessary. You shouldn't expect to use the virtual memory capability often, but it's nice to have when you need it. For example, suppose your computer has 256 kilobytes of RAM. If the program takes up 90 kilobytes of internal memory, you have approximately 166 kilobytes for your spreadsheet before you begin accessing virtual memory, enough for rather large reports.

A computer with a hard disk speeds up the disk accessing process. If your program is hard disk compatible, that means you can copy it from a hard disk machine's floppy disk drive to the hard disk for enhanced program operation. Copy-protected programs may or may not allow this, but they certainly won't allow you to make floppy disk copies of your program. Backup copies either come with the program, or are supplied by the vendor.

2. Vendor phone support is one of the most important considerations when selecting a program. Even when the documentation is excellent, situations may arise that make access to comprehensive technical expertise a necessity. Some vendors will refer you to your dealer for assistance, but this is seldom a productive route to follow. Some vendors offer an advisory service for a monthly or yearly fee.

Documentation

1-3. Documentation usually is provided in the form of a user's manual in a loose-leaf binder, and may be augmented by online help. Poor documentation is a common problem, even with the best software. Unless you have enough experience with software to be able to fill in the gaps left by incomplete instructions, you'll be wise to examine the documentation of any prospective program very carefully. Frequent diagrams, illustrations of screen displays, and color highlighting of important items are signs of good organization and attention to detail.

Be sure that page numbers, chapter headings, and section titles are clear and easy to locate. Indexing is rarely satisfactory, so a comprehensive table of contents and glossary take on special importance. A command reference section at the back of the manual should be augmented with a pull-out reference card listing often-used commands.

Look for a *tutorial* in the manual. A tutorial is a progressive series of lessons, and a good tutorial section should cover all (or nearly all) program features. Some vendors will provide a tutorial on disk that demonstrates key aspects of spreadsheet operation. Disk tutorials can be excellent, but they should not bear the entire burden of program instruction.

The better disk tutorials involve you in question-and-answer situations, and even prompt you to issue commands. This is a desirable feature, but sometimes the questions are too narrowly defined and block experimentation with the program. A stronger type of instruction includes a detailed printed tutorial augmented with sample files on disk. In many cases, you actually modify these sample files and build a report, step by step, from an empty matrix to a finished template.

Your program should be designed for minimum error occurrence, smooth error recovery, and maximum user assistance. Most user errors are the result of mistyping. A program that uses the IBM PC keyboard effectively is likely to invite fewer typos than one that ignores keyboard potential or uses it poorly. Look for a program that makes intelligent use of special keys, like the functions keys F1 through F10. To aid in the use of the special keys, some manufacturers supply *keyboard templates*. These are usually plastic stick-on caps or covers cut to fit over the keyboard, with labels identifying individual keys.

Good programs have straightforward error recovery procedures, beginning with error messages that appear onscreen when problems arise. Error messages should be written in clear, unambiguous terminology, and the manual should contain a section (usually an appendix) that lists all error message and error recovery procedures. Programs that give error messages in the form of codes and vague generalities can cause a great deal of user frustration. Onscreen error messages should also include a brief description of the recovery action to be taken—for example, "File not found: press ESCAPE to continue."

Screen Characteristics

The information a spreadsheet displays and how that information is arranged onscreen are two of the most important aspects of user interface. Second-generation spreadsheets vary widely in the size, flexibility, and clarity of the reports they display. Use this section of the Checklist to help you determine which programs pay proper attention to screen design.

1. Begin by estimating the approximate number of columns and rows in your average report. Then double this figure to determine the minimum you'll need in a spreadsheet program. At first glance, most second-generation spreadsheets may seem to offer many more columns and rows than you need. But keep in mind that a larger matrix affords you flexibility in the arrangement of your report, as well as allowing for subreports within a single matrix.

2. The way in which you access different parts of a report directly affects the efficiency of report construction. Most spreadsheets allow cursor jumps to individual cell addresses, a definite need in the case of reports that extend beyond the borders of the screen. When you move the cursor around the report a lot, you'll find it convenient to keep the titles of the rows or columns "locked" onscreen while the data scroll in relation to them. If your reports require lengthy titles, a "title spillover" function will let you extend titles continuously across more than one cell.

3. Multiple windows are an advantage when your report invites comparison of two or more sections at a time. A screen that can be split into two windows will allow you to compare, for example, a graph in one window, with its corresponding figures in the other. Four windows could allow you to view sections of four quarterly reports at once. The ability to scroll windows in unison ("synchronously") or independently ("asynchronously") gives you added flexibility when viewing and comparing data.

4. A convenient way to organize subreports is to place them on separate pages of a three-dimensional spreadsheet. Pressing a single key (usually the Page Down key on the IBM PC keyboard) will display each succeeding page in turn. One advantage of page organization is that the same relative cell positions can be used on each page for the same data. For example, sales figures for June, 1984 may be in column A of the first page, the figures for June, 1985 in column A of the second page, and so on. When you switch pages, you'll see the same month for a different year without having to do any tricky scrolling.

5. Because of size restrictions, a well-designed screen should not be cluttered with too much extraneous information. At the same time, a good spreadsheet should let you know at a glance how much memory you have left, and the filename of the report in which you are working. Information like this is usually located on a status line at the top or bottom of the screen. The addition of certain key indicators (e.g., Caps Lock and Num Lock) to the status line helps reduce entry errors. When a color monitor is in use, color highlighting of screen elements can also help overall clarity.

For some purposes, such as clear display of a graph, elimination of the coordinates at the top and side of the screen is desirable. Being able to hide coordinates is also handy when using the IBM PC keyboard's Print Screen key to send a screen display directly to the printer.

6. At various stages in program operation, most spreadsheets will prompt you with a question asking for the necessary information to complete an operation. These "user prompt messages" help guide you through various program functions. "Forms mode" allows your spreadsheet template to act as an electronic version of a standardized paper business form. Designed primarily for use by data entry personnel, this feature restricts cursor movement to selected cells of a template and in a predetermined sequence.

Editing Functions

There are two basic editing functions for a spreadsheet program. First, you should be able to correct a typing error quickly and easily while making an entry. Second, you should be able to modify an earlier entry without needing to erase it and start over again.

1. If you expect to use lengthy text labels and comments or fairly complex mathematical formulae, you'll appreciate a strong set of cell editing features. The ability to edit cell contents is a must for anyone that makes mistakes. Some programs will also let you set the cursor to move to the next entry position (up, down, left, or right) by pressing the Return key.

2. Aside from editing individual cell entries, other spreadsheet editing functions provide large scale copying, erasing, and transferring operations that greatly facilitate report and template development. Skilled operators working with a variety of report styles will look for a full complement of these commands. You should be able to copy or move the contents of a block (range) of cells as well as those of single cells. Copying the cell format only and replicating the contents of one cell across a block of cells are refinements that should be expected in a second-generation spreadsheet.

3. If you expect to develop your own templates, you'll appreciate the flexibility afforded by the ability to delete and insert columns and rows. Another feature that aids in template experimentation is a "clear report" command that lets you erase everything in your current workspace, without requiring you to restart the program.

4. When you want to make changes for What If...? modeling, the ability to move directly to a cell that contains a particular item of data is a great time saver. Facile spreadsheets support various kinds of search functions that will put the cursor where you want it. With a "tab search" function, you set an item of data as your target and press the Tab key. If you do not set a particular target, pressing the Tab key will move you to the next cell containing data of any kind. "Global search and replace" finds an expression and automatically replaces it with a new one throughout the report.

5. Spreadsheet operators who are not computer-oriented are often attracted to spreadsheet programs that allow you to replace cell references in formulae with English cell names. For example, if the total of a column of figures resides in cell C36, that cell may be named TOTAL. The English name may then be used in formulae that refer to cell C36. A formula like (C36 + 100), may be written (TOTAL + 100) instead. This capability is akin to variable names used in programming languages like BASIC and Pascal. An extension of the same idea allows English range names for whole blocks (ranges) of cells.

Standard cell references often turn out to be more convenient to use than their English counterparts. Far from being cryptic, a reference like A12 is a very precise description of a cell location. However, the overall clarity of a template can be enhanced by using English names as variables in important formulae—especially if the template is large and complex.

Cell Formatting

Unlike a paper spreadsheet, the displayed value in a cell on an electronic spreadsheet may not be literally the same as the entry. This is particularly obvious in the case of a formula entry: The displayed value is the result of the formula, not the formula itself. How should a formula result be represented in the cell? That depends upon the purpose of the report. The more types of data you include in your reports, the more cell formatting options you need.

1. If your report uses large figures, it will benefit from "automatic commas" (1,000,000 instead of 1000000). For money amounts, you'll appreciate a dollars-and-cents format ($1,000,000.00). Inexperienced personnel and slow typists will be particularly grateful for the simplification afforded by these formatting options. In addition to dollar sign and automatic comma formats, bookkeepers and accountants will be interested in credit/debit notation, parentheses for negatives, and the ability to align numbers at the decimal point.

2. Spreadsheet programs make a sharp distinction between text entries and numeric entries. Without dollars-and-cents formatting, an entry like $10.00 would have to be entered as text and could not be used in calculations. This is because the dollar sign itself is a text character and not part of the number. A few spreadsheets allow mixtures of text and numeric entries in the same cell. This feature offers enhanced flexibility and speed of data entry, although excellent templates can be designed without it. If you expect to create templates for data entry personnel, you'll want to have cell protection to prevent accidental erasure of formulae.

3-6. A typical spreadsheet will automatically align numeric entries at the right side of the cell (right justified) and text entries at the left side (left justified). Usually, spreadsheets also offer a standard two-decimal format, with a cell width ranging from 9 to 12 characters. These default settings can become cramped very rapidly.

In compensation, better programs will provide left, right, and center justification, as well as "center titles" formatting for centering major headings horizontally or vertically on the screen. If your reports include lengthy text entries, the ability to adjust the width of columns individually is essential. A large number of entries that exceed standard width settings may be accommodated by adjusting the column width globally.

   7. Graphics format allows a numeric value to be expressed as repetitions of a selected character. Some programs limit this formatting option to a repeated letter that yields a primitive kind of bar chart. Others allow you to specify one of the many graphics characters available on the screen. This will permit better screen graphics, but the resulting chart will not print on paper as it appears on the screen unless you also have some command over printer control codes (more on this in the following section). Note that a simple graphics format capability is not the same as a full set of graphics functions found in integrated graphics software.

   A "display formulae in cells" option allows you to inspect the spreadsheet with the formulae showing in place of the calculated values. When you create or modify your own templates, this feature can help in analyzing the template structure. The "hide cell contents" option, which prevents display of a calculated result, can be a useful option when certain cells hold formula results that don't need to be displayed. If your spreadsheet allows you to adjust row height, you can extend the cell size vertically within a given row.

   8. If your program has global formatting options, you can set selected cell formats for the entire spreadsheet. Among such formats are usually those for "fixed decimal" (specifying the number of decimal places to be displayed), "percent format for decimals" (e.g., displaying 50% instead of .50), "scientific notation" (which displays in powers of 10), and "integer format" (which allows display of whole numbers only). Note that integer format is not the same as rounding to the nearest decimal.

Print Formatting

The relationship between your spreadsheet report and its printed counterpart is determined by print formatting features. For some purposes, such as carrying out certain calculations or viewing graphed results, a printer may not be necessary. In general, however, it's the printed report, or hardcopy, that must be considered the primary output of the spreadsheet program. One of the great virtues of electronic spreadsheets is that presentation quality printed reports can be generated quickly and efficiently— including graphics, if the program supports an appropriate printer and/or a plotter.

   1. If you want to print high-impact reports or specialized business forms such as invoices, checks, and so on, you should look very carefully at the kind of printing capability provided by the program. A good spreadsheet program will include a printer installation program that allows you flexibility in adjusting a printer to produce what you want in hardcopy. Others also have printer setup strings offering enhanced control over the look of your printout.

   2. For better graph reproduction on a dot matrix printer, you'll need printer control codes for specific printing effects. Your printed reports can be given an extra impact by italic, expanded, or boldfaced type if your program allows you to use alternate fonts. If your program has a "print formulae" feature, you can generate a printed listing of the formulae used to create the report template—a valuable feature for those who create their own.

A spreadsheet report will not always fit neatly on standard 8½ by 11-inch sheets, so the program must provide print options that allow you to specify how the report will be divided. Some spreadsheet programs allow you to print the current screen display. If the part of a report you wish to print can be contained on a single screen, the "print screen contents" feature is an easy way to generate hardcopy. This is particularly true if your program includes title centering commands and other formatting features that enhance the onscreen appearance of the report. The ability to turn off the display coordinates improves the appearance of a report printed in this manner. When you use a print screen command, you can print split screens (windows) that you may not be able to print using standard printing commands.

3. The "print partial report" feature lets you identify a particular block of cells and send that block to the printer as a unit. If the program will print a report in separate pages, then you can configure selected columns and rows to a standard page size with sequentially numbered pages. The ability to fit output to paper affords additional control. Generally, such capabilities are geared toward onscreen formatting, where the report prints out essentially the way you have developed it on the screen. Occasionally, however, titles will have to be specially treated in order to obtain a printout exactly like the screen display.

When a spreadsheet program includes a report generator, you write out a list of commands to control the printout instead of formatting the report on the screen. For example, your screen display may not show a centered title, but the title will be centered on the printed copy. Some programs combine elements of report generation (e.g., headers, footers, and special titles) with regular onscreen formatting.

The separation of the spreadsheet program from the printing process reaches its extreme in a program that requires a word processor for proper formatting of titles, pages, margins, and so forth. Although a report generator or an external editor is less immediate, either may be able to offer more sophisticated printed copy. Making a decision between the two approaches to printing will depend upon the balance between your desire for immediate results and your need for text-oriented printouts. If your reporting requirements are extremely demanding, you may want to consider a program that is integrated with, or can share files with, graphics and word processing programs.

File Handling

A file is a collection of related information stored on disk. Spreadsheet reports are saved in separate files, and are retrieved by a command that reloads them into the workspace. On a basic level, file handling involves file storage, deletion, and copying. Programs that can exchange files with other programs or that can link saved spreadsheet reports add significant versatility to spreadsheet operation.

1. The drive containing the disk used for file storage is called the logged drive. If you are using a hard disk system or you expect to use more than two floppy disk drives, it's convenient to have a program that allows you to specify the logged drive.

2. The command that writes a file to a disk is usually called Save, and the command that reads a file from a disk is called Load. These are basic file-handling operations and are taken for granted in any spreadsheet program. You will gain flexibility if the program will both read and save partial reports. You also should expect to find Copy file, Delete file, and Rename file commands. These operations can be carried out by returning to the operating system and using the operating system's equivalent commands, but a good program should provide them as a contribution to your convenience and efficiency.

3. The specific way that report data are written to a file is called the file format. Some spreadsheet programs offer a choice of file formats, the most common of which is a "universal" format called ASCII. If you want the option of transferring spreadsheet data to and from a word processor or text editor for report preparation, then your spreadsheet program should be able to read ASCII files.

Some programs read and save files in a specialized ASCII configuration that supports data exchange with certain other programs as determined by the manufacturer. Such formats are DIF (VisiCalc's Data Interchange Format), SDI (SuperCalc's SuperData Interchange), and SYLK (Multiplan's Symbolic Link). DIF and SDI are essentially the same and have become an informal standard that can be read and saved by many of the newer programs. Files in these formats also may be transmitted by modem.

4. Since it's often useful to connect separately filed reports, various means for report linking have been developed. The simplest is a "merge files" command that combines the contents of a filed spreadsheet with those of the spreadsheet currently in memory. Merging two files is like superimposing one upon the other. The superimposed spreadsheet retains all its data, overwriting most information on the one "beneath" it. Only empty cells in the "top" spreadsheet will allow information from the "bottom" spreadsheet to show through.

A more useful form of report connection is the "consolidate report" feature. This allows you to merge two reports by adding together the data in superimposed cells. Consolidation capabilities may be extended by commands that link individual cells or link several different reports. Note that a three-dimensional spreadsheet offers particularly efficient report linkage, since linked or consolidated reports may be placed on different pages of the same spreadsheet, rather than in separate files.

Recalculation

Recalculation is the backbone of a spreadsheet's What If...? capabilities. When you change or make additions to the underlying figures in a projection, most spreadsheets will recalculate the dependent series of operations automatically. Quick revisions in projected scenarios make spreadsheets a truly interactive modeling tool.

1. Automatic recalculation updates the spreadsheet after every single entry. In a large report, however, this can slow down operations, since you have to wait for the recalculation cycle to finish before you can make the next entry. To avoid such delays, a spreadsheet should have a "manual" option that suspends automatic recalculation and recalculates only when you ask for it.

Some spreadsheets use simple linear recalculation. This process starts from a given point (usually the first cell) and proceeds stepwise one cell at a time, by row or by column. With linear recalculation, speed and accuracy can be affected by the way you design the template. Forward references, or calculations that depend upon the results of formulae in cells not yet reached by the recalculation sequence, and circular references, or mutually dependent calculations, can cause inaccuracies or slowups. The ability to specify calculation by columns or calculation by rows gives you added design flexibility to help overcome such difficulties.

2. Natural recalculation, unlike linear, orders the calculation sequence according to the natural dependencies of the formulae. Iterative recalculation allows you to select the number of passes made through the template. Some forms of iterative calculation allow the calculation cycle to repeat until a specified limit is reached in a given cell. A spreadsheet featuring natural and iterative recalculation gives you greater freedom in template design and minimizes problems of forward and circular reference.

Mathematical & Trigonometric Functions

A second-generation spreadsheet should present you with a strong group of mathematical functions. These should extend well beyond standard addition, subtraction, division, multiplication, and exponentiation.

1. You'll typically find program functions that return the square root or the sign of a number, raise to a power, and perform modulo arithmetic (yield the remainder after a division). Standard relational operators used for the construction of formulae, such as equals, greater than, and less than, are provided as a matter of course.

2. Trigonometric functions found in advanced spreadsheets include logarithm, tangent, cosine, sine, and in many cases arc tangent, arc sine, and arc cosine. There are minor variations from spreadsheet to spreadsheet, and if a particular function is of special importance, you should take these variations into consideration. Some spreadsheet programs contain radian/degree conversion and random value functions, while others do not. Rounded value and the ability to put "Pi" in your formulae as needed are also not necessarily standard functions.

3. One of the special features of some newer programs is that they provide shortened forms of simple mathematical operations (such as addition), as well as a rich selection of advanced trigonometric functions. For example, to calculate the sum of a number of cell values, all you need to use is the "sum of a list" or SUM function. SUM(G10 to G60) will give you the sum of fifty cells without having to write out all the cell references connected by plus signs. Other functions that smooth out report building for the non-mathematician are integer value, rounded value, absolute value, and random value. There are also several handy functions of this kind among the Financial and Statistical functions described in the next section.

Financial & Statistical Functions

Thanks to the financial and statistical functions now included in spreadsheet packages, desktop spreadsheet power is overtaking that of mainframe financial modeling languages. Many of the generally available functions support sophisticated financial modeling, while the preprogrammed statistical functions make it easier for non-mathemeticians to use a spreadsheet effectively.

1. Sophisticated financial functions like future value, which calculates the value of an investment at a given interest rate for a given time period, can save you a great deal of time if your templates require the kind of values they return. Many such functions calculate important values for assets, investments, and loans—such as net present value, internal rate of return, payment, depreciation, annuity, and interest.

For example, if you wanted to display the present value needed to develop a future value of $15,000 invested at 13 percent per year for eight years, a present value function would allow you to enter the relevant data into a formula to deliver the result—in this case, $5,642.40.

2-3. Clever use of functions like average value, maximum value, minimum value, count items in list, and modal value (most frequently occurring value in a list) can result in remarkably useful templates with a minimum of mathematical know-how. Imagine that you have a range of cells containing employee zip codes and you have given the cell range the name ZIPS. The modal value function could be used to determine the area where the majority of the employees live. The formula would be very simple: MODE(ZIPS). More advanced statistical functions such as sum of squares, standard deviation, regression analysis, and variance are available on some spreadsheets, but not all.

Logical & Specialized Functions

Data management functions have greatly augmented the electronic spreadsheet's utility. Most second-generation spreadsheets also offer an array of logical functions, which increase your control over spreadsheet operations by offering commands sets that resemble a rudimentary programming language. In addition, the inclusion of date and time functions offers convenience when generating time-sensitive reports.

1. Alphabetic and numeric sorting are the two most elementary data management functions. "Choose" and "Lookup" are more sophisticated. The Choose function picks the Nth value from a list of values, while the Lookup function searches a table for a value matched to a specific data classification. A simple Lookup function finds a match between values in adjacent columns. Some three-dimensional spreadsheets have Lookup features that match values in adjacent columns, rows, or pages.

By careful use of cell references, the values returned by these functions can be made to depend upon the results of other calculations. For example, taxable income can become a data classification in a tax table for a Lookup formula that returns the amount of tax. The income itself may be calculated by the template on the basis of financial information entered for that purpose. By varying the data, the Lookup formula will draw tax information from the table according to different income possibilities, providing you with a What If...? tax analysis. Functions like these are powerful spreadsheet replacements for what would otherwise be complex programming tasks.

2. Logical functions allow the use of conditionals in formulae. When a formula using "if...then" is calculated, the result in the cell depends upon whether or not a given condition elsewhere in the report is true or false. It is possible to develop a full set of logical relations using only nested conditionals and the "not" operation, but this is doing it the hard way. If you are untrained in the use of logical relations, make certain your spreadsheet program includes "and," "or," "not," and nested conditionals, as well as the more flexible "if...then...else" form of the conditional.

3-5. If you enter a date or a time in your spreadsheet report, you'll have to treat the expression as a text entry rather than as a numeric entry unless the program supports date and time calculations. If the program has a function that displays the current date or time, these can be automatically included on such documents as invoices without having to type them yourself. Such functions may allow you to display today's date, display the time of day, display the day of the week, and calculate "duration" (i.e., the interval in days between dates). Spreadsheets that calculate date or time intervals (usually in days and minutes) are especially valuable when the spreadsheet program can exchange data with a time management program.

Integrated Features

Electronic spreadsheets began with an emphasis on calculation—thus the expression "calc" in names like VisiCalc, SuperCalc, Calcstar, and many others. However, second-generation spreadsheets reflect an ongoing experimentation with expanding capabilities.

1-4. Many newer programs use spreadsheets as a core around which graphics, database management, word processing, and data communications applications are added. These integrated features often provide enhanced convenience and speed, but they should be scrutinized carefully before making a purchase. For instance, the "database management" capability advertised by a spreadsheet program may turn out to be a few simple sorting and Lookup functions. Or, a built-in "word processor" may turn out to be an elementary text editor. A true word processing interface will allow you to include spreadsheet data within a text report with enhancements like footnotes, underscoring, and so on.

If you're uncertain about the degree of integration you need, you might want to consider a spreadsheet program that can simply share files easily with other applications, and also has a few integrated features like internal graphics formatting, list sorting and Lookup functions, and a good set of editing commands.

5. The "keystroke macro" is an elementary kind of internal programming capability. Keystroke sequences are recorded in cells of the spreadsheet, then automatically executed either upon issuing a special command, or in some cases upon loading the program. This capability may be expanded by the addition of programming commands that provide for conditionals and subroutines, to create an "internal programming language." One valuable use of an internal programming capability is to create an automated report form (for example, in invoicing) that can be filled out easily by an inexperienced person with no knowledge of the spreadsheet command system.

6. Electronic spreadsheets can be enhanced by added programming capacity. Any spreadsheet that can save report data in ASCII format (including DIF and SDI formats) already has the capacity to exchange data with a programming language like BASIC. You can write a BASIC program to read spreadsheet data from the ASCII file, manipulate the data in ways more appropriate to BASIC, then write the results back into an ASCII file to be read again by the spreadsheet program and displayed as a spreadsheet report. However, this requires a number of steps that can be avoided if the spreadsheet contains a built-in programming language of its own.

Part II

Electronic Spreadsheet Software

Chapter 4

Reviewing
the Benchmark
Products

The phenomenal speed and power of electronic spreadsheets helped launch the microcomputer revolution. Spreadsheet software made the personal computer a low-cost, powerful tool for solving business problems.

As the number of micro spreadsheet users rapidly increased, however, so did the number of suggestions on how to improve this new business tool. Soon more and more programmers were busy trying to top one another by producing new, sophisticated spreadsheet products that featured a complete array of mathematical, statistical, financial, logical, and other useful business functions.

This chapter addresses the demand for enhanced microcomputer spreadsheets by exploring, in depth, two of the most popular programs produced to date: Multiplan, from Microsoft Corporation, and 1-2-3, from Lotus Development Corporation.

Based on two divergent approaches to number crunching and problem solving, both Multiplan and 1-2-3 are well-established, second-generation spreadsheet programs with a loyal following of users.

Two basic criteria establish a program as a benchmark. First, it must occupy an "historical" position in the software market. That is, the products presented here are not necessarily the best available, but they set an industry standard by establishing important features imitated by many subsequent spreadsheet programs. Second, a benchmark must have a substantial share of its market. Both Multiplan and 1-2-3 qualify handily in this regard.

To give you a hands-on feel for using a spreadsheet, the reviews here will explore program features in detail, from basic commands and screen characteristics, to high-level financial and statistical functions. The differences between the two benchmarks receive special emphasis, giving you an idea of each program's style. In this way, you'll see how the general descriptions of speadsheet functions found in earlier chapters apply to specific products. A good understanding of the benchmark products will also serve as a yardstick for evaluating the programs reviewed in Chapter 5.

Each review in this book begins with a Fact File box containing basic product information. This includes a listing of the operating system (or available systems) and computer hardware you'll need to operate the software product, the general parameters of the spreadsheet program matrix, compatible programs and data exchange formats, and the product's listed retail price. (Additional comments on the interpretation of each fact in these boxes can be found at the beginning of Chapter 5.)

Multiplan

COMPANY:	Microsoft Corporation
REQUIREMENTS:	PC-DOS, MS-DOS, CP/M; 64K; one disk drive.
LIMITS:	255 rows; 63 columns.
COMPATIBILITY:	Microsoft Chart, Microsoft Project, VisiCalc (Software Arts); reads SYLK files.
PRICE:	$195

Chosen by *InfoWorld* magazine as the software product of 1982, Microsoft Multiplan moved into the enviable position of overall best-selling microcomputer program for 1983. Among IBM PC programs, it was second only to Lotus Development Corporation's integrated spreadsheet package, 1-2-3. With its reliability, ease of use, and low cost, Multiplan remains one of the best spreadsheet values on the market.

At first glance, Multiplan may seem to exhibit a few deficiencies, compared with some of the latest spreadsheet programs. For instance, the program offers a notably small matrix (254 rows by 63 columns) as well as a relatively slow speed of calculation. But in selecting an appropriate software package, it never pays to judge a program without taking a closer look.

In the case of Multiplan, you may discover—as many other business users have found—that Multiplan is just right for your particular set of needs. For example, if your available RAM is limited, Multiplan requires only 64K of internal memory. In addition, the program makes up for its small matrix by letting you link different spreadsheet files.

Furthermore, Multiplan's clear and concise command structure rivals that of any spreadsheet program on the market. If you can get along without such enhancements as flashy graphics and keyboard macros, Multiplan's well-designed features and functions may provide you with just the spreadsheet capabilities you need.

Program Installation

Multiplan requires only 64K of RAM. If your equipment has under 128K of internal memory, however, parts of the program are left on the disk and used only as needed. This means that Multiplan will access the disk more frequently, slowing down program operation.

Starting Multiplan requires a number of disk formatting and copying activities. The disk of sample files (for use with the tutorial sections of the manual) is copied using the DOS DISKCOPY utility. A one-time working copy of the program is made with the assistance of a copy program called

MPCOPY, and two special files, MP.HLP and MP.SYS, are copied to a data disk using the DOS COPY command.

These installation procedures are not difficult, but they do demand careful attention, especially from those who are unfamiliar with DOS file copying operations.

General Characteristics

The Multiplan screen opens a 7-column by 20-row window on a 63-column by 255-row matrix. Columns and rows are numbered, so that "R12C5" is the cell reference for "Row 12, Column 5" instead of the more commonly found E12 for "Column E, Row 12." This method of cell referencing demands a minimum of four keystrokes to type a cell address, compared to a minimum of two keystrokes for the letter/number method. As a result, formulae in Multiplan are longer and have a more complex appearance.

Letter/number method: (E12 + A4)
Multiplan: (R12C5 + R4C1)

The complex appearance of Multiplan formulae is heightened by the program's method for expressing relative cell references (described later under "Functions & Formulae").

In addition to the row/column location of the cursor, the screen displays a variety of basic information, including the filename of the currently loaded model and the percentage of free memory available for that model. Just above the location indicator at the bottom left of the screen is a message line that supplies a prompt for the current situation. Above that resides a menu of relevant command options. Figure 4-1 shows the menu of command options that appears onscreen at startup.

Multiplan's screen is uncluttered, but some users also find it a bit oversimplified. You won't find Caps Lock or Num Lock indicators, color highlighting for enhancing screen status information, or an option to hide screen coordinates. These limitations are in keeping, though, with the "no nonsense" character of the program.

On the other hand, you can split the display screen into as many as eight windows and scroll them synchronously or asynchronously. The program also offers both title locking and title spillover. In addition, if your computer system utilizes an 80-column color monitor, you can "paint" windows different colors for better visual impact.

Although Multiplan's graphics are severely limited, the program does provide a graphics cell format for simple bar charts made up of asterisks. A special function called REPT lets you create bar charts using any screen-printable ASCII character. In addition, the program communicates with a graphics package, Microsoft Chart, for full graphics capability.

Basic Command Procedures

In using Multiplan, you enter commands by typing the first letter of any displayed command option, or by moving the cursor to the selected option on the command line and pressing the Enter key. In the entry mode, pressing the F10 key or the spacebar moves the cursor forward, and F9 moves it backward. Experienced spreadsheet users generally prefer pressing the first letter of the command name, simply because it's faster.

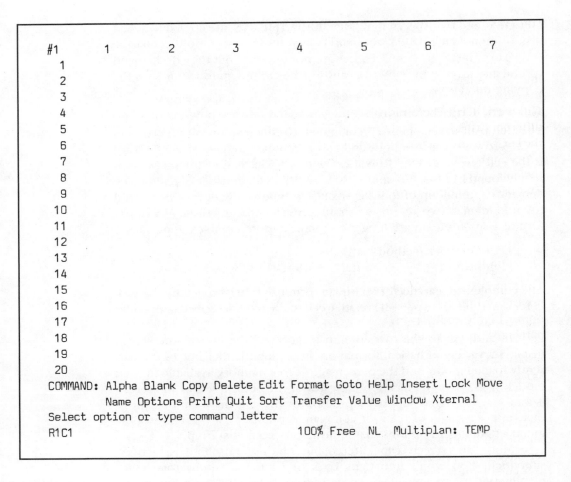

```
#1        1         2         3         4         5         6         7
 1
 2
 3
 4
 5
 6
 7
 8
 9
10
11
12
13
14
15
16
17
18
19
20
COMMAND: Alpha Blank Copy Delete Edit Format Goto Help Insert Lock Move
         Name Options Print Quit Sort Transfer Value Window Xternal
Select option or type command letter
R1C1                                     100% Free  NL  Multiplan: TEMP
```

FIGURE 4-1 Multiplan Startup Screen

Since Multiplan's default is the command mode, you don't need a special prefix to initiate a command sequence. Slash command programs such as VisiCalc, on the other hand, require that you press the slash key to go into the command mode—a significant stylistic difference.

Multiplan has a treelike command structure. Finding your way through the "branches" of the command tree is fairly easy, because the options for each level are spelled out on the screen in a clear, step-by-step manner. This onscreen clarity, however, exacts a price in terms of keystrokes.

Suppose, for example, that you want to give the active cell a fixed-decimal format to three decimal places. From the menu of primary commands, you first select Format by pressing the "F" key. The program then presents you with a list of subcommands, which includes: Cells, Default, Options, Width. To select the Cells option, you press the "C" key, thus moving further down the command tree to a list of sub-sub commands. The command line now displays the following items:

Format cells: R1C1   Alignment: (Def) Ctr Gen Left Right
Format code: (Def) Cont Exp Fix Gen Int $ * %   # of decimals: 0

Considering the way you ordinarily select options from a command line, you might try typing "F" to activate the Fix option, or try moving the cursor to the option by pressing the spacebar. But neither of these moves will work here. The options on the command line are now divided into different categories called "fields," and you must use the tab key to move the cursor from one field to the next. This requirement makes the Multiplan procedure relatively cumbersome. Not only are more keystrokes required, the entry "rhythm" is trickier and requires more attention to the screen.

Here's a comparison of keystrokes needed for the same command in three different spreadsheet programs (1-2-3, Report Manager, and Multiplan):

1-2-3 (6 keystrokes):	/RFF3 Enter
Report Manager (5 keystrokes):	/FF3 Enter
Multiplan (8 keystrokes):	FC Tab Tab F Tab 3 Enter

The Multiplan procedure is actually more practical for beginners, since the use of both the tab and letter keys makes selection of a wrong command option highly unlikely. In the long run, however, it's slower than the comparable slash command technique.

Data Entry & Cell Formatting

Since Multiplan is normally in command mode, you must remember to change to entry mode before entering information into a cell. Text entry mode is initiated by the Alpha command, and numeric entry mode is activated either by the Value command, a digit from 0-9, or any of the characters for the plus, minus, equal, left parentheses, quote, or period symbols. For repeated text or numeric entries, Multiplan remains in entry mode as long as a cursor movement key is used to terminate each entry.

If you forget to make the proper preparation for a text entry, you may accidentally issue a command causing unwanted results. For example, suppose you forget to initiate entry mode and begin entering the label "Quantity" but type Qy for the first two letters instead of Qu. Unfortunately, Multiplan will interpret your keystrokes as the Quit-Yes command, and you'll end up exiting the program and losing any unsaved material in your file.

Multiplan offers an adequate array of functions for editing cell contents. The F7, F8, F9, and F10 function keys direct cursor movement, and the Backspace and Delete keys fulfill their usual editing roles. You can delete entries by character or by word. Some confusion may arise onscreen or in the manual regarding the difference between text and formula editing, but a few trials will make the procedure clear.

The command for clearing the workspace is included, oddly enough, under the Transfer command options. Multiplan cannot search the worksheet for a specific text or value, but the F2 key moves the cursor to the next (unlocked) cell that contains an entry.

There's also an automatic cursor-direction feature that expedites entry of a row or column of figures. You can easily move or copy cell ranges and individual cells. When copying formulae, both absolute and relative modes are available (also described later under "Functions & Formulae").

Multiplan offers most of the essential numeric cell formats, such as dollar sign, automatic commas, scientific notation, and so forth, and it permits global cell formatting. Labels in cells may be justified-left, justified-right, or centered, and cell protection also is provided. However, one formatting omission may hamper accounting applications: There is no credit/debit notation and no provision for parentheses around negative numbers. Multiplan also lacks decimal justification for aligning columns of numbers by decimal point.

The graphics format displays a bar of asterisks in a cell, which corresponds to the numeric value of the cell entry. Unfortunately, the maximum cell width is 32 characters, severely limiting the scale of a bar chart. You can, however, use the Format Cells Continuous option to obtain title spillover, which lets you stretch a single cell across several columns.

Print Formatting

For a quick printout of part of a model, you can send a single screen display to the printer by pressing the Print Screen (PrtSc) key. For longer reports, there are four print subcommands that let you set the top and bottom margins to suit your paper length, indicate the part of the worksheet you wish to print, and print to a disk file instead of the printer.

A printer setup option allows you to specify printer control codes for compressed characters, double-width characters, emphasized type, double-strike, and more. You can save control codes with the worksheet so they'll be in effect the next time you print. Multiplan also lets you enter control codes directly into cells for printing individual labels, titles, or other data, according to your specifications.

If you have a serial printer, an appendix in the user's manual gives instructions for making the correct adaptation. Other spreadsheets have more printing features, but Multiplan provides enough flexibility to print clear, attractive reports without necessitating the use of a separate, word processing program.

File Handling

Multiplan can save, load, overwrite, delete, and rename files from within the program, but it has no file copy or merge commands. The program cannot read standard ASCII files, but it can read VisiCalc and SYLK (SYmbolic LinK) files. SYLK files contain all of the information needed to reconstruct an entire Multiplan report, including formulae. The information is stored in ASCII code, so SYLK files can be both read and written by user-developed programs. Multiplan's manual says almost nothing about SYLK files, however, except for the information contained in a terse and overly technical appendix.

You can link different spreadsheets through the Multiplan's eXternal Copy command. The program manual terms the spreadsheet supplying data the "supporting" sheet, and the one receiving data the "dependent" sheet. When you load the dependent sheet into the workspace, it automatically receives data (not including formulae) from the cells or cell ranges you've designated in the supporting sheet. You can only transfer the data to blank cells of the dependent sheet, but Multiplan does not support adding, subtracting, or multiplying data across linked sheets.

If you establish a chain of dependent sheets, intermediate sheets in the chain must be loaded before the final sheet will be updated. This makes updating slow in comparison to more dynamic sheet linkages available in other programs. Three-dimensional spreadsheet programs (reviewed in Chapter 5) offer superior linkages between multiple "pages," each as large as a single Multiplan matrix.

Multiplan includes an interesting eXternal Use command that lets you name an alternate supporting sheet without having to dissolve the current linkage setup and create new links. For example, you could prepare individual summary sheets for different years by using a single dependent sheet as a template.

Functions & Formulae

Practically all of the mathematical and trigonometric functions outlined on the Needs Assessment Checklist (in Chapter 3) are available in Multiplan, except for Random Value, Arc Sine, Arc Cosine, and Radian/Degree Conversion. Multiplan is relatively weak in preprogrammed financial functions, supporting Net Present Value only. However, a template allows you to calculate Internal Rate of Return using the spreadsheet's powerful iterative capability.

The iterative recalculation feature of Multiplan is backed up by two special functions, DELTA (maximum of absolute values in cells from one iteration to the next) and ITERCNT (current iteration count during the iteration phase). Examples in the user's manual illustrate how to use these functions for financial modeling.

The program provides statistical functions for Standard Deviation, Maximum Value, Minimum Value, Count of Values, and Average Values. You can also implement the logical functions "and," "or," "not," and "if...then...else" (with nested conditionals allowed). The only data management functions supported are Lookup and Sort (alphabetic and numeric, ascending and descending). There are no date or time functions.

Multiplan has several commands for manipulating strings of text, including a Repeat function that can create bar graphs using any available screen character. You can also use special IBM graphics characters—such as the half-tone bar—with the repeat function by typing the ASCII number on the numeric keypad while holding down the Alternate key.

When a cell entry is a mathematical formula, only the result of the formula is calculated and displayed in the cell. Cell references act as variables in formulae, taking on the current value of the referenced cell. For example, if the cell at Row 3, Column 1 contains the number 36, the formula "R3C1 X 2" will place a result of 72 in the cell containing the formula.

You also can use relative cell references in formulae. For example, the cell reference R[+ 4]C[− 2] denotes the cell four rows below and two rows to the left of the current cell.

Multiplan includes an automatic formula-building feature. During formula entry, the program will put any desired relative cell references into the formula if you move the cursor to the referenced cell. You can convert a relative reference to an absolute reference by pressing the F3 key.

Relative cell references are especially valuable when you want to copy formulae from one part of a template to another. This preserves the same pattern of mathematical relationships among the cells, but not the same absolute references. Some spreadsheets, like Multiplan and 1-2-3, distinguish between relative and absolute cell references at the time you enter the formula, fixing the pattern to be copied. Other spreadsheets (such as InteCalc and Report Manager, both reviewed in Chapter 6) use only one type of cell reference in the formula, but allow you the flexibility of specifying which type you want copied each time you issue the copy command.

Multiplan recalculates upon loading and after every entry unless you turn off the automatic recalculation option, at which point you may recalculate the worksheet on demand by pressing the F4 key. The mode of recalculation is natural: The program selects the order of cell calculation according to the mathematical dependencies that have been established. Written in the ''C'' programming language, Multiplan is generally slower at calculation than assembly language programs such as 1-2-3, SuperCalc, and VisiCalc.

Circular references (i.e., formulae with results that depend on each other) must be taken into account when building templates in Multiplan, but an iterative calculation option is available that can help overcome unresolved circularity. In spreadsheets without an iteration option, you might have to recalculate an unknown number of times before achieving the desired degree of accuracy. With Multiplan, recalculation is repeated automatically until the solution to the problem becomes less than a predesignated amount.

User Assistance

In keeping with its concern for beginners, Multiplan supplies excellent context-sensitive help screens. Pressing the Alternate and ''H'' key simultaneously displays information on the currently highlighted command option. You can also scan the help file for any other command information you may need. Figure 4-2 shows a sample help screen.

Multiplan handles errors well. When errors occur, clear indicators like ''Name too long'' or ''Cannot link those windows'' appear on the message line, accompanied by an (optional) acoustic alarm. The manual includes a 14-page appendix of error message explanations that analyzes the cause of each error and offers the appropriate recovery procedure.

In addition to error messages, calculation errors of various sorts are signaled by specific cell displays. For example, if you attempt to use an undefined name, the cell will display ''#NAME?''. For the most part, error recovery in Multiplan is a simple affair that can be completed without reference to the program manual.

The Multiplan user's manual is fair, but not exceptional. It's divided into four main parts: ''Getting Started,'' ''Tutorial Section,'' ''Reference Section,'' and a section containing five appendices.

The Tutorial section is supported by various sample files on disk, an example of which is shown in Figure 4-3. Screen illustrations in the manual, many showing sample files, are printed in very small, light green type and are difficult to read.

```
format code:
        Choices are:

Def     Format as specified by the Format Default command.

Cont    Continues long text across column border, if next cell
        empty and also formatted "Cont".

Exp     (Scientific notation) Displays numbers as a decimal times a
        power of ten. Number of digits as specified in "# of decimals."

Fix     Rounds to and displays number of decimals specified
        in "# of decimals" field.

Gen     (General) Displays numbers in the most appropriate form
        considering the size of the cell and of the number.

Int     Numbers will be shown as integers after rounding.



HELP: Resume Start Next Previous
      Applications Commands Editing Formulas Keyboard
Select option or type command letter
R1C1                                    100% Free  NL  Multiplan: TEMP
```

FIGURE 4-2 Multiplan Help Screen for Format Code Options

The tutorial is also plagued by frequent gaps in explanation that assume too much on the part of the user. Some important features are almost impossible to discover except by accident—such as the useful fact that a readout of available memory seems to appear as a "side effect" of the Options command.

Unfortunately, the examples provided in the command reference part of the user's manual are generally poor. Perhaps the best section of the manual is the first reference chapter, "Elements of Multiplan." This chapter gives the most coherent and complete explanations, particularly those regarding key usage. The manual index is sketchy at best.

Other user aids include an unwieldy but informative fold-out reference card, and a smaller card that rests above the keyboard as a quick guide to special keys. Multiplan also offers limited telephone support.

Summary

Multiplan represents a significant improvement over first-generation spreadsheets. It is low in cost, easy to use, and a reliable performer. Installation is somewhat complicated, but well explained. The command structure is cumbersome, yet should be attractive to beginners because of its clarity and error resistance.

The program's automatic formula construction and the capacity for naming cells and cell ranges in formulae facilitate template construction. The list of preprogrammed functions, though weak in financial applications, includes a good set of mathematical, statistical, and string-handling functions as well as logical operations and sorting. Iterative recalculation and two supporting functions allow for creation of more complex financial modeling templates.

```
#1          1       #2      2         3         4         5         6
 1                          January   February  March     April     May
 2
 3 Sales                    $20000.00 $20200.00 $20402.00 $20606.02 $20812.08
 4
 5 Cost
 6          Material        $5000.00  $5040.00  $5080.32  $5120.96  $5161.93
 7          Labor           $7000.00  $7000.00  $7000.00  $7000.00  $7000.00
 8          Overhead        $4000.00  $4032.00  $4064.26  $4096.77  $4129.54
 9                          ------------------------------------------------
10      Total Costs         $16000.00 $16072.00 $16144.58 $16217.73 $16291.47
11
12
13
14
15 Gross Profits            $4000.00  $4128.00  $4257.42  $4388.29  $4520.61
16
17
18
19
20
COMMAND: Alpha Blank Copy Delete Edit Format Goto Help Insert Lock Move
         Name Options Print Quit Sort Transfer Value Window Xternal
Select option or type command letter
R3C3      RC[-1]*101%                  94% Free  NL  Multiplan: SPENCER6
```

FIGURE 4-3 Multiplan Sample File Screen

Multiplan is not an integrated spreadsheet program. It has a very limited graphics capability and doesn't accommodate keystroke macros. The matrix size is also limited, but a provision for linking worksheets helps overcome this limitation. Although the Multiplan user's manual has numerous shortcomings, the program's overall user-friendliness, plus a tutorial disk of sample files, make it possible to learn Multiplan without outside help. In addition, a number of books devoted entirely to Multiplan are currently available (see the Bibliography in Appendix C).

1-2-3

COMPANY:	Lotus Development Corporation
REQUIREMENTS:	PC-DOS, MS-DOS; 192K; two disk drives or hard disk.
LIMITS:	2,048 rows; 230 columns.
COMPATIBILITY:	dBASE II (Ashton-Tate), VisiCalc (Software Arts); reads ASCII, DIF files.
PRICE:	$495

1-2-3 is an integrated package that combines a powerful spreadsheet with business graphics and a limited set of database management functions. Only three months after its release in early 1983, 1-2-3 topped the list of best-selling IBM PC programs. Since then it has maintained its position as the dominant spreadsheet product.

There are several reasons for 1-2-3's popularity. One is precedence: 1-2-3 was within a few months of being the first integrated package available for microcomputers, and it certainly benefited from the biggest marketing blitz the microcomputer software industry had seen. More important, 1-2-3 had the features and functions to back up the publicity. Users found it fast, easy to learn, and easy to use. The program also has a large matrix, and a substantial array of built-in functions.

In 1984, Lotus Development Corporation introduced Symphony, an enhanced version of 1-2-3 that includes word processing and data communications applications. Although Symphony was released with a great deal of fanfare, many users have indicated that they still prefer the original version. As a result, 1-2-3 appears likely to maintain its superior standing among spreadsheet products for quite some time.

Program Installation

1-2-3 is not particularly easy to install. Five different disks are involved: a system disk, a system backup disk, a utilities disk, a tutorial disk, and a graphics disk. A special program called INSTALL assists you in the installation process. If your system runs DOS 1.1 and contains more than 320K of internal memory, you must use a program called FIXDOS (included in the package) to make required corrections to two DOS programs, DISK-COPY and DISKCOMP.

Hard disk installation requires the DOS Copy and Erase commands. The printer interface default is parallel, but you can change this setting to serial by using an option under the Worksheet Global Default command. The program will support up to two printers, provided they are both parallel, or both serial.

When you have finished installing the program, typing the startup command "LOTUS" will move you to a general, umbrella-like menu called the Lotus Access System, which is shown in Figure 4-4. From this menu, you can select any of the three programs that make up 1-2-3 proper—that is, 1-2-3, PrintGraph, and Translate— as well as disk management and file management utilities.

```
Lotus Access System  V.1A  (C)1983 Lotus Development Corp.        MENU
-----------------------------------------------------------------------------
1-2-3  File-Manager  Disk-Manager  PrintGraph  Translate  Exit
Enter 1-2-3 -- Lotus Spreadsheet/Graphics/Database program
=============================================================================




                         Tue  01-Jan-80
                         0:37:51am






          Use the arrow keys to highlight command choice and press [Enter]
      Press [Esc] to cancel a choice; Press [F1] for information on command choices
```

FIGURE 4-4 Lotus Access System Menu

You can also enter 1-2-3 directly from DOS by typing "123". In either case, startup is impossible without a factory copy of the program disk in the A drive. Lotus does supply a backup copy of the program disk, but you cannot make additional fully functioning copies.

General Characteristics

1-2-3 references cells by column letter and row number in the manner first established by VisiCalc. D24, for example, is the absolute address for the cell at column D, row 24. As soon as you've started up the program, 1-2-3 displays a window of 20 rows by 8 columns out of a possible 2,048 rows by 256 columns. The full matrix contains 524,288 cells.

Over half a million cells seem immense in comparison to Multiplan's full matrix of 16,065 cells, but it is by no means the largest spreadsheet available. A more important question is: How many of these cells can you actually use?

For instance, on an IBM PC-XT with 256K of internal memory, if you repeated a single, three-digit number in each cell, the maximum matrix you could utilize would amount to 32,768 cells—about 94 sheets of standard size paper. When formulae are added, this figure shrinks rapidly. According to one report, an internal memory of 544K was exhausted at approximately 19,000 cells by a template of moderate complexity.

Aside from the cell pointer and the column and row coordinates, the only indicators on the screen at startup are the current cell address at the top left, and a mode indicator at the top right. The contents of the active cell, if any, are displayed on the top line following the cursor location indicator. 1-2-3 stays in entry mode—with the mode indicator reading "READY"—until you initiate a command with the slash key. The mode indicator turns red and blinks "WAIT" during command processing. 1-2-3 also provides Caps Lock, Scroll Lock, Num Lock, and End key indicators at the lower right corner of the screen.

Most users find that the information provided as part of 1-2-3's display screen looks sparse. Coordinates are not enhanced by color, and there's no automatic display of memory status or of the current report filename. You can, however, obtain additional status information by typing the Worksheet Status command "/WS." As shown in the upper part of Figure 4-5,

```
                       Label    Column   Avail                      MENU
       Recalculation   Format   Prefix   Width    Memory   Protect
   AUTO      NATURAL    (G)       '         9      138230   OFF
          A         B         C         D        E        F        G        H
   9
   10
   11
   _____

   A1:                                                                MENU
   Worksheet  Range  Copy  Move  File  Print  Graph  Data  Quit
   Global, Insert, Delete, Column-Width, Erase, Titles, Window, Status
          A         B         C         D        E        F        G        H
   1
   2
   3
```

FIGURE 4-5 1-2-3 Worksheet Status Display & Primary Command Menu entering this command displays the current recalculation mode, column width, available memory, and other information at the top of the screen. Pressing the Escape key returns you to entry mode.

You can split the screen into two windows, either vertical or horizontal, and you can scroll them synchronously or asynchronously. Forms mode, cell protection, and title locking are available, along with a spillover feature that automatically extends extra characters into adjacent cells. A nice feature of the 1-2-3 screen is its versatile scrolling and cursor movement capability. In addition to using the arrow keys to control cell-by-cell cursor movement, the F5, Home, End, Page Down, Page Up, Tab, and Scroll Lock keys provide a variety of ways to move quickly and conveniently to any desired area of the matrix.

Basic Command Procedure

Issuing 1-2-3 commands is a simple, straightforward procedure. You enter the command mode by pressing the slash key, which causes the word "MENU" to appear as the mode indicator. In this mode, two lines at the top of the screen act as a command line and a message line. The command line gives the current command options, which are selected in the usual manner by moving a highlighted cursor to the desired command name and pressing Enter, or by typing the first letter of the command. You move the cursor from option to option with the left or right arrow keys.

The message line displays the available subcommands for the currently highlighted option. If there are no subcommands, the message line explains the highlighted command's function. You can't select a subcommand until you actually enter a command from the command line. The bottom part of Figure 4-5 shows the primary command menu as it appears when the first option, Worksheet, is highlighted. Only the first line of options shown in the Figure is active.

The subcommand procedure varies from option to option. For example, after typing "/WGFF" (Worksheet Global Format Fixed), the program prompts you with: "Enter number of decimal places (0..15): 2." This prompt appears on the command line. It tells you the number of decimal places currently displayed in all cells. To change the current format, you type a new number and press Enter. The computer records the new format and then returns to entry mode. If you choose to press Escape instead of making an entry, you'll move back to the previous menu of options. Pressing the key several times returns you to entry mode.

Data Entry & Cell Formatting

1-2-3 remains in entry mode unless you press the slash key. The program does, however, require you to differentiate between numeric entries and labels. Number or formula entries must begin with any of the characters for the digit, plus, minus, period, left parentheses, at (@), number (#), or dollar sign.

For a label entry (such as the word "Total"), you just type the word and press Enter. Pressing an arrow key instead will both enter the label (i.e., "Total") and move the cursor to the next cell in the direction indicated by the arrow.

The program provides several useful features for both numeric and label entries. For example, typing a percent sign after a number automatically displays that number in percent format. Typing an apostrophe, a caret, or a double-quote *before* the label entry causes the label to be either left-justified in the cell, centered, or right-justified. Typing a backslash (\) before the label will cause it to be repeated up to the cell's border.

If you make a mistake during the entry process, you can "back up" using the destructive backspace, or press Escape and cancel the entry. An unprotected entry in a cell can be overwritten by any new entry. If a block of many cells requires changing, you can use the Range Erase command to blank all the cells in the range before making new entries.

For more detailed editing, you can move the cursor to the appropriate cell and press F2 to activate the edit mode. This causes the current cell entry to appear on the command line, where you can move from character to character using the left and right arrow keys. You can make corrections in the characters by using the Backspace, Delete, and Insert keys. The tab or backtab keys will move the edit cursor five characters at a time left or right, while the Home and End keys move the cursor to the beginning or end of an entry, respectively. The variety of edit cursor movements contributes to editing speed. However, 1-2-3 lacks Multiplan's ability to erase an entire word or formula element at a time.

You can move, copy, replicate, or assign English names to cells or cell ranges. Columns or rows can be deleted or inserted, and clearing an entire report is executed using the Worksheet Erase command. 1-2-3 does not support tab search or global search-and-replace functions, but you can use the data management and macro capabilities of the program to accomplish certain search procedures.

1-2-3 aligns all numeric entries at the right side of the cell, and cannot be formatted for decimal, center, or left justification (except for label entries as noted above). The program cannot center titles on the screen, hide cell contents, or display graphics characters. Credit/debit notation isn't available, but you can give negative numbers a parenthetic format. The program also supports both global and individual cell formatting.

Formatting a cell range entails entering a range expression, such as A1..C15 (where A1 and C15 are taken as diagonal corners of the range), or by moving the cell pointer from one corner of the range to the other. The highlighted area of the cell pointer expands to mark the entire range. This is a convenient, fast, and vivid way to define a small range area.

Print Formatting

1-2-3's print files can be read by most word processing systems, allowing you to edit a report extensively before printing. However, the program tailors reports by itself quite well, using its own print formatting functions. These options include headers, footers, and horizontal or vertical borders, along with selected page margin lengths. You can print cell entries as displayed or as a listing that includes formulae. The unformatted option suppresses any preset headers, footers, and page breaks, and you can specify and print multiple ranges as part of a single printing operation.

The Worksheet Global Default commands allow you to control printer configuration. For ease of normal use, you can specify default settings for all of the following items: serial or parallel interfacing, automatic line feed, page margins, page length, pause for paper change, and printer setup strings (control codes for the printer).

During Print command procedure, you can also specify individual setup strings that override default settings. 1-2-3 makes it easy to enter print control codes by using the backslash followed by the appropriate ASCII number of the code. For example, the control code combination that produces italics on an Epson printer (designated as Escape 4) is entered as "\0274". The manual provides a handy appendix with a complete ASCII code table and instructions for creating printer setup strings.

Instead of using the standard Print command to print graphs, you must save graphs in special files for later printing via the PrintGraph program, which is part of the Lotus Access System. To print a graph, you must leave the spreadsheet, return to the access system, and select the PrintGraph option.

File Handling

1-2-3 has two separate file-handling facilities: those provided by the Lotus Access System, and those provided by the spreadsheet module. From within the spreadsheet, the Worksheet Files command allows you to store, list, retrieve, and erase worksheet files. You can also save a partial worksheet (a specified range of cells) as a separate file by using the program's File Xtract option. Since you may develop 1-2-3 models larger than disk capacity in the workspace, the Xtract option is particularly valuable for saving large worksheets in sections.

1-2-3 doesn't link or consolidate separate files, but you can create the equivalent of several files in different areas of the worksheet, save them separately with the Xtract command, and then combine them again in a single worksheet with the Combine command.

Like many other spreadsheet programs, 1-2-3 reads ASCII text files, which basically includes word processing files and files arranged in sequential data format. ASCII files generated by other programs must be renamed with the file extension ".PRN" (for print file) before they can be used by 1-2-3.

Other file management functions are handled through the Lotus Access System. A Transfer utility converts VisiCalc worksheets, DIF files, and dBASE II files to 1-2-3 format, while the Access System File Manager lets you copy, erase, and rename files. A disk directory listing appears when you use the Access System File Manager. You can use the Sort option to arrange this directory onscreen in alphabetic order, in order of file date, and so on. An Archive feature lets you copy a specified group of files under new names for backup purposes. In addition to the File Manager, a Disk Manager provides formatting, copying, comparing, and disk status reporting.

Functions & Formulae

You can use cell references in 1-2-3 formulae, and both individual cells and cell ranges can be assigned English names. A dollar sign before a cell reference or a name makes the reference absolute rather than relative.

1-2-3 goes even further than some spreadsheet programs by allowing *mixed cell references*—that is, the column may be absolute and the row relative, or vice-versa. For example, C7 and $TOTAL are absolute references; C7 and TOTAL are relative references; and $C7 or C$7 are mixed references.

The program lets you enter cell references into formulae automatically by moving the cursor to the desired cell during formula building. The cell reference will be in relative form, but you can change it to absolute or mixed form by pressing the F4 key one or more times.

Standard mathematical and logical operators, including "and," "or," and "not," can be used in 1-2-3 formulae. With the exceptions of Radian/Degree Conversion and Sign of Value, 1-2-3 supports every one of the mathematical and trigonometric functions listed in Chapter 3's Needs Assessment Checklist. Two arc tangent functions, two-quadrant and four-quadrant, are available.

1-2-3 also supports five preprogrammed financial functions: Internal Rate of Return, Net Present Value, Future Value, Present Value, and Payment. The statistical functions, including Count, Sum, Average, Minimum, Maximum, Standard Deviation, and Variance, all have database counterparts that operate on values in 1-2-3 database fields.

Five date functions cover the years 1900 through 2099. Dates are entered and calculated using December 31, 1899 as a reference point, making calendar arithmetic easy to perform. A special date format option will display dates in any of three standard ways: 01-Jun-85, 01-Jun, or Jun-85. The program has no time functions.

1-2-3 function names are preceded by the @ sign to distinguish them from text entries. For example, the conditional function "if...then...else" would be represented by @IF(Condition,X,Y)—that is, the value for X will be placed in the cell if the condition is true, and the value for Y if the condition is false. The program also allows nested conditionals.

Other logical functions in 1-2-3 include @TRUE, which returns a zero (0), and @FALSE, which returns a one (1). Two special functions include @ERR, which simulates an error condition, and @NA, which simulates a "value not available" condition. Two logical functions, @ISNA(x) and @ISERR(x), return the value True when the values of X are not available or in error, respectively. These functions allow you to detect not available or error conditions in a specified cell.

The Worksheet Global Recalculation command offers either automatic or manual recalculation of the worksheet, iteration to a desired number of repetitions (up to a maximum of 50), and recalculation in natural order, column-wise order, or row-wise order.

At startup and each time the worksheet is erased, the default setting is for automatic recalculation in natural order. A nice feature of the program is that any circular references in formulae will trigger a "CIRC" warning message onscreen. In addition, a "CALC" indicator appears on the screen whenever you have the program in manual recalculation mode. Pressing the F9 key invokes manual recalculation.

Integrated Features
Unlike Multiplan, 1-2-3 is a full-fledged integrated package. As mentioned earlier, the total program includes a formidable spreadsheet, graphics, data management, and programmable keyboard macro functions.

Granted, 1-2-3's graphic output looks primitive in contrast with advanced spreadsheet graphics, such as those produced by SuperCalc3 (from Sorcim/IUS Micro Software). However, 1-2-3's graphs are perfectly adequate as personal decision tools. You can graph data using any one of five methods: line, bar, stacked bar, pie, and two (X-Y) axes. An automatic scaling feature tailors graphs to fit the screen, but you can also set graph scales manually. Graphs can represent values in up to six ranges at once (in a line graph, this means up to six lines), and you can enter labels into graphic displays.

Graph values are tied to cell ranges, which makes What If...? graphing merely a matter of changing the data in these ranges, and then pressing the F10 key to view the graph. Pressing F10 a second time returns you to the spreadsheet. Graph settings, which include the graph type and the ranges to be charted, are saved with the spreadsheet. As previously mentioned, printing a graph requires that you use the PrintGraph option in the Lotus Access System.

The keyboard macro facility lets you record a series of keystrokes in a cell or a column of cells, and then activate these keystrokes on command. For example, you can enter the keystroke sequence for the Worksheet Global Format command by simply typing "/WGF." Non-printing keys, such as the arrow keys or the Escape key, must be entered with surrounding curly braces—for instance: {Esc}. Another special symbol, ~ (the wavy line or tilde), represents the Enter key.

As a specific example of the type of macro command you can create, the following sample line would send the cell pointer to cell C6, widen the column to 15, and name the text entry "Total:"

{GoTo}C6 ~ /GCS15 ~ Total ~

You can place long keystroke sequences (like the above sample line) in more than one cell of a column, and label the top cell of the column with a special name. The name of the cell must be made up of a backslash followed by a letter. Whenever you want to activate a macro, you merely press the Alternate key and the assigned letter key simultaneously.

The advantage of using keystroke macros is fairly obvious: You can speed up the development of a template significantly, particularly in cases where similar operations must be repeated a number of times. You can set up a macro sequence to pause for input, creating user-interactive templates. A special group of commands, including a conditional and a Goto command, turns the macro capability into an internal programming language, letting you construct fully automated spreadsheets.

As for 1-2-3's database function, although it doesn't approach the power of a dedicated database program, it's still a valuable feature— especially when combined with the spreadsheet's macro capabilities and statistical functions. Like all data management applications, the 1-2-3 database stores data in tabular form. You can extract this data selectively by using various sorting, organizing, and querying commands.

A 1-2-3 database is made up of spreadsheet rows and columns: Each row holds a single record, and each record is divided into one or more sections called *fields,* represented by a single cell in that row. The Data Query command lets you pick out any group of records and fields from the database according to your own preset criteria.

To use the Data Query command, the top cell in each column must be given a label called a *field name*. A mailing address record, for example, might contain such field names as: Name, Address, City, State, and Zip. Each field of the database would occupy one column of the spreadsheet.

1-2-3's Data Query command includes four basic operations, and pressing the F7 key automatically repeats the most recent data query operation. These operations include: Find, which locates specific records; Extract, which copies selected fields of specified records; Unique, which eliminates duplicate records; and Delete, which deletes specified records.

1-2-3 includes two special data management functions, Lookup and Choose. The Lookup function allows both horizontal and vertical table lookups, where the comparison values are either in the first row or the first column of the designated range, respectively. You can use the Choose function to test logical expressions, or use it to perform short table lookups.

You can perform statistical analyses of selected database records and fields by using the special statistical functions, which include: Sum, Average, Variance, Count, Standard Deviation, Maximum Value, and Minimum Value. Other useful data management commands include Data Sort, which arranges data in ascending/descending or alphabetic/numeric order; Data Distribution, which obtains the frequency distribution of data in a given range; and Data Fill, which fills a range of cells with numbers in a predetermined sequence. This last command is particularly useful when building tables.

User Assistance

The chief claim-to-fame for 1-2-3 user assistance is the program's disk tutorial, an interactive program that introduces the user to the program's capabilities and conventions. The tutorial is divided into six lessons, two of which are devoted to database and graphing. The lessons are rigid (you have no leeway in making answers and no freedom to experiment) and the tone is condescending, but there's no question that the tutorial gives you a clear-cut, comprehensive introduction to 1-2-3.

Without the tutorial on disk, a beginner would have to rely on the user's manual. That would mean a slow, difficult learning period, mostly because of the manual's abysmal organization. The section of the manual on installation, for example, is quite confusing. The chief difficulty lies in the way implementations for a two-disk system and a hard disk system have been jumbled together. A very small pamphlet, "Getting Started," is supplied as an aid to installation, but this pamphlet contains less information in the same order found in the manual. The "Configuring 1-2-3" appendix offers little extra help.

Unfortunately, the manual is typeset in inexcusably small print, particularly in the case of screen illustrations. Typography and headings are ineffective in helping you follow the logical order of commands. The explanations of the various preprogrammed functions and the examples used with them are particularly weak. The indexing is skimpy and badly arranged, with many important topics missing or buried in inappropriate places.

In its favor, the manual is printed on slick, high-quality paper, and features two levels of indexing tabs at the margins for quick location of general topics. Cursor movement and scrolling procedures are carefully described in the "Basic Skills" section. A well-made plastic template, designed to remind you of the operations assigned to the function keys, adds to the documentation package. Lotus also provides a 12-page quick reference booklet that lists commands, function keys, filename procedures, special keyboard uses, all mathematical functions and operators, editing keys, and other useful features. A vendor newsletter is available for a fee.

Like Multiplan and most other high-quality spreadsheet programs, 1-2-3 provides a number of context-sensitive online help screens. Pressing the F1 key leaves the command line and the message line onscreen, while filling the remainder of the screen with the appropriate portion of the help file. Figure 4-6 shows the help screen for the Column Width option.

```
A1:                                                                  HELP
Global   Insert  Delete  Column-Width  Erase  Titles  Window  Status
Set display width of the current column
MMMMMMMMMMMMMMMMMMMMMMMMMMMMMMMMMMMMMMMMMMMMMMMMMMMMMMMMMMM 124;142 MMMM
Worksheet Column-Width -- Set the display width of current column

D 1. Choose to Set column-width explicitly or to Reset to the global width.
  2. (Set only) Specify column width (1-72), by adjusting visually
         or by typing a number.

Resetting the width of a column returns it to using the global column-width.

When you change the global column-width (Worksheet Global Column-Width), 1-2-3
automatically adjusts:

y Columns whose widths you have never Set individually, and

y Columns whose widths you have Reset.


DDDDDDDDDDDDDDDDDDDDDDDDDDDDDDDDDDDDDDDDDDDDDDDDDDDDDDDDDDDDDDDDDDDDDDDDDDDDD
Next Step---Set         Next Step---Reset
Troubleshooting        Numeric Display Formats
Worksheet Commands     Worksheet Global Column-Width   Help Index
```

FIGURE 4-6 1-2-3 Help Screen for Column Width Options

While 1-2-3's help facility is extensive, the help screens themselves are cluttered and usually require you to make further menu selection before you find the desired information. The program also does not allow you to explore the entire help file at any time, as does Multiplan.

1-2-3 is good at handling errors. An audible tone alerts you that an error has been made, and error messages are generally informative and specific—for example: "Disk is write protected" or "Directory does not exist." An appendix explains all error messages and recommends corrective action.

Lotus offers free telephone support, although its technical support number is not toll-free. Support personnel are generally cooperative and knowledgeable, and the amount of time you may have to wait for a representative has decreased considerably since the company's early days.

Product Summary

1-2-3 is undoubtedly the most popular spreadsheet program in history, and one of the best-known programs in the entire microcomputer industry. Scores of businesspeople who don't even use microcomputers seem to have heard of this software product. In fact, you'll typically find more books on 1-2-3 than on any other software product in most computer bookstores. In this book alone, the Bibliography (see Appendix C) lists 20 separate books devoted to explaining, understanding, and using 1-2-3.

Yet 1-2-3 does have its drawbacks, not the least of which is its price. The program is also rather difficult to install, and its documentation is poorly organized. For those who need extensive spreadsheet linkage, three-dimensional spreadsheet programs (reviewed in Chapter 5) might be a possible alternative.

All facts considered, however, 1-2-3 is a powerful integrated spreadsheet program with great speed of operation, a large matrix, and a wide range of mathematical, statistical, and logical functions. It also includes effective database capability, macro programming, and graphics.

Chapter 5

Surveying the Competition

This chapter presents several of the leading spreadsheet software products currently in use. These programs were selected for their ability to meet the basic needs of most business users. They also provide a diverse selection of program styles and enhancements, and represent some of the latest or most popular programs on the market today.

As you study the spreadsheet programs in this chapter, you'll find a wide range of prices and sophistication. Some of these products are well-known best sellers, while others are still trying to define and capture their share of the business market. All of the programs, however, incorporate enough enhancements to qualify as second-generation spreadsheets.

Presented alphabetically, each entry begins with a Fact File box that contains the product name and publishing company, system requirements, program limits and compatibility, and price tag. The requirements statement lists the operating system(s) available, as well as the minimum memory and disk storage your computer system will need.

Limits refers to the maximum number of rows and columns in a spread-sheet's matrix. In the case of three-dimensional spreadsheet programs, a third parameter delimiting the maximum number of pages also appears.

Compatibility deals with two considerations. First, it refers to any additional software that can interface with the reviewed product. For example, some software publishers offer a series of stand-alone programs that can be linked together to share data files. Some also allow you to "import" files from specific programs produced by other vendors. In this latter case, the vendor name is indicated in parentheses following the name of the compatible program.

Second, the compatibility statement shows the file transfer formats supported by the program. The two most common formats are ASCII, used by word processing programs, and Data Interchange Format (DIF), originally developed for VisiCalc. Support of these and other file transfer formats allow a spreadsheet to share data with a multitude of other applications.

Price refers to suggested retail price, but it's not unusual to find significantly lower prices than the publisher's list price if you shop around.

After the brief Fact File, you'll find a basic review and evaluation of each spreadsheet product. Each discussion explores essential program characteristics, along with any outstanding strengths and weaknesses. The reviews also comment on intended markets, ease of use, and performance.

Each product's documentation is examined, including the user's manual, reference cards, keyboard templates, online help screens, and tutorials or sample lessons (if included). Good documentation is crucial in teaching you how to use a spreadsheet program effectively.

The information provided in these reviews is based on test results from actual business users who applied the evaluation criteria presented in Appendix A. In Chapter 6, you'll find a comprehensive series of tables comparing all of the spreadsheet programs reviewed in this book. For even more information on the programs mentioned and on additional spreadsheet products, use the directory of software publishers listed in Appendix B.

Finally, although most of the language used in this part of the book has been explained earlier, you may find it helpful to consult the Glossary for quick and concise definitions of terms.

Aura

COMPANY:	BPI Systems, Inc.
REQUIREMENTS:	PC-DOS, MS-DOS; 256K; two disk drives or hard disk (recommended).
LIMITS:	255 rows; 63 columns.
COMPATIBILITY:	BPI Accounting Software, dBASE II (Ashton-Tate), 1-2-3 (Lotus Development Corp.); reads ASCII files.
PRICE:	$595

Aura is a popular integrated system that features four business software programs: spreadsheets, data management, word processing, and business graphics. Unlike most integrated packages, however, Aura does not use one application as a foundation on which the others depend. In fact, each of these programs is strong enough to be marketed as a stand-alone product.

Although Aura's spreadsheet has only à 63-column by 255-row matrix, it makes up for its small size with several outstanding features. Among these are the ability to link spreadsheets through the program's special Zoom and Xreference functions, the option to retrieve data from information management for manipulation in a spreadsheet report, and the power to add graphics within a spreadsheet and print it using Aura's graphics application. In addition, Aura has more than 50 mathematical, trigonometric, logical, and financial functions.

Various features now commonplace qualify Aura's spreadsheet as a solid second-generation program. You can sort values in ascending or descending order by column or row. You can use English names in formulae or assign them to spreadsheet cells or ranges and adjust column width as needed. A simple command displays formula entries, and you can protect cells or hide cell contents at will.

An external reference option, called Xreference, provides report consolidation. It allows you to build links between cells in two different spreadsheet reports, or between spreadsheet reports and Aura database files. When a file that has been linked to another file is updated, corresponding fields on the second file automatically reflect the changes.

The spreadsheet uses the same type of cell referencing as Multiplan. R17C3, for example, refers to row 17, column 3. Most people find this method cumbersome, especially when constructing formulae. Controlling the cursor is easy, however, since the program makes good use of the IBM PC arrow and function keys.

Aura's spreadsheet features a command menu at the bottom of the screen, and a description appears on a separate line as each command is highlighted. Help menus, accessed by pressing F1, are abundant. If you precede F1 by the Control key, a screen appears that describes the keys used for cursor movement within the spreadsheet, editing within cells, and other information (e.g., the function keys used to recalculate, clear the grid, and Zoom).

To enter text, you must type a quote or double quote both at the beginning and at the end of the entry. Many operations require long sequences of keystrokes. For example, to format a cell with a dollar sign in it could require as many as eight keystrokes: You would type "E" for edit; press Enter; type "D" for display; press Enter again; choose the cell, rows and/or columns you wish to format; select the video attribute (optional) and alignment (optional); press the End key; select "cell format $"; and, finally, press F3 to make the entry.

To share files with other programs, BPI provides a utility called the Aura Reformatter that converts files from specific programs into a form readable by Aura. Designed specifically to convert BPI Accounting Software, 1-2-3, and dBASE II files, the Aura Reformatter will also read ASCII files.

The Aura package includes two large manuals, a reference guide, a tutorial, a well-designed reference card, and a keyboard template. There's also a disk of sample files which are used in the tutorial.

While generally well-organized and well-written, the manual is a bit sketchy when dealing with more complex functions like Zoom and Xreference. The tutorial might have helped in this instance, but the sample files disk didn't contain all of the data it should have. Discrepancies in the documentation also appeared. For example, although the reference guide states that only uppercase letters show onscreen, both uppercase and lowercase letters are, in fact, displayed.

Program installation is not a simple task. It requires copying each of nine disks in a specified sequence onto newly formatted disks, or onto a hard disk. You cannot start Aura unless you complete this installation procedure. If you want to duplicate only one disk, you must copy all the disks preceding it in the original duplication sequence.

Tailoring the program for your particular system during installation is fairly easy, and the process is menu driven. The menu offers a number of popular printer choices, including Okidata 83A, Epson MX-80, IBM Graphics Printer, IDS Prism, and Florida Data OSP 130.

Most spreadsheets allow you to divide the display into windows to view different portions of a report at one time. Aura doesn't provide this capability. Likewise, Aura won't let you shunt among its four applications without shutting down one before moving onto another.

Aura has two other major drawbacks, the worst being that the package is supplied on nine separate disks (11 disks including the sample data disk and the Aura Reformatter) and requires frequent disk swapping unless used on a hard disk system. If you're using the program on a floppy disk system, you may find yourself switching disks too often to really make the program's integrated abilities worthwhile. For instance, one user reported having to switch disks three times to enter the program and retrieve a spreadsheet.

Aura is also relatively slow. In one test, it took the program several minutes to format about 200 rows with dollar signs. Saving a file is time consuming, and moving to a new location in the spreadsheet can be tedious. If you move the cursor from R17C5 to R1C1, for example, data is re-entered on the screen one cell at a time, from left to right across the rows.

In comparison with 1-2-3, Aura does fairly well. The program's database is more sophisticated and, unlike 1-2-3's database, it's not limited by total system memory. Aura's graphics program allows you to draw your own free-form diagrams, and its word processor features block manipulation, search and replace, multiple document editing, and layout and print controls.

Although Aura's spreadsheet is much smaller, it has almost all of the same functions as 1-2-3, plus the ability to sort rows and columns and create graphs. While not as powerful as some programs, Aura's spreadsheet has the calculating functions, keyboard macros, and sheet-linkage capabilities to make it a fine, competitive program.

Framework

COMPANY:	Ashton-Tate
REQUIREMENTS:	PC-DOS; 256K; two disk drives or hard disk.
LIMITS:	30,000 rows; 30,000 columns.
COMPATIBILITY:	dBASE II, dBASE III; reads ASCII files.
PRICE:	$695

Framework is the well-known integrated software package that includes programs for database management, word processing, spreadsheets, graphics, and data communications. It's also the first integrated product that lets you automatically organize information from each of its applications into an outline. As a result, many users contend that Framework is the only complete office management package that appeals as much to word people as to number crunchers.

In Framework, the term "frame" has more than one meaning. Depending on the context, it can refer to a window, a file, or an application. You can bring more than one frame (file) into view at a time, and the number of frames that can be displayed simultaneously is determined by your computer's RAM capacity.

Using the function and arrow keys, you can move frames around the screen, reduce or enlarge them, and place frames within other frames. You can even put a frame in a "tray" at the bottom of the screen, temporarily, to get it out of the way. All of these activities are quick and easy to perform.

From a mode called Outline View, you can enter and rearrange information under sections and subsections of a basic outline form provided by the program. You can insert and delete sections (the items are re-numbered automatically), move them, sort them in ascending or descending order, and create secondary subsections.

In Frame View, you can go into the frames, designate them as spreadsheet, word, graph, or database frames, and enter the appropriate text or numbers to create the actual document. Back in Outline View, the corresponding sections and subsections are flagged to indicate the type of frame they represent. The letters S, W, G, D, and E are used to signify spreadsheet, word processing, graph, database, and empty frames.

A complex document can be made up of many pages of graphs, tables, and narrative. From Outline View, you can see the relationship of one section to another, and you can find a particular portion of a document without searching through the file itself. For example, if you want to work on the second chapter of a report, you can locate it in the outline and open its frame with a touch of the F10 key.

Theoretically, the Framework spreadsheet matrix has a maximum size of 32,000 rows by 32,000 columns. In reality, however, the maximum practical matrix size is much smaller; in fact, Framework lends itself to small, closely linked spreadsheets. When you create a new spreadsheet report, you must specify the number of rows and columns to be allocated. Later, if your estimate turns out to be wrong, you can easily enlarge or reduce the matrix. This method saves memory and disk space, and can make your spreadsheets more manageable.

Framework uses the standard method of referencing cells: Columns are labeled alphabetically, rows numerically. You can move the cursor cell by cell in any direction, skipping empty cells if necessary. You can also move row by row, column by column, to the beginnings/ends of columns and rows, and to the top/bottom of the spreadsheet itself. Framework is missing a Goto cell command, but the Locate command used in the program's word processing mode works in spreadsheet frames too, enabling you to search for a particular entry.

Text entries are recognized automatically. If you begin a text entry with a number, you must press the spacebar first to indicate that the number should not be calculated. If you enter a formula that begins with text, you must press the F2 (Edit Formula) key first or the program will interpret it as a text entry.

The spreadsheet provides a full array of mathematical, trigonometric, logical, financial, and statistical functions. Among the missing functions are depreciation, annuity, interest on loan, and sum of squares. Date and time functions and nested conditionals are included. The spreadsheet handles both forward referencing with automatic recalculation, and manual recalculation by row or column order.

Framework lets you link spreadsheet reports with databases or graphs. You can reference an entire database field category from a spreadsheet cell using the program's cell pointing feature. Graphs, which are drawn from previously created databases and spreadsheet reports, are automatically and permanently linked to their sources. As a result, any changes made to the source are reflected in the graph.

Framework allows you to create keyboard macros which are stored in individual frames, making them equally available to each of the applications. This provides an advantage over 1-2-3 macros, for example, which are accessible only from the spreadsheet in which they reside.

Another nice feature of the package is the FRED programming language. It allows you to add functions not already built into the program using its own set of values, references, and operators. You can also set up your own data entry routines, and even create custom-made menus.

The Framework package comes with a tutorial manual and a reference manual. The tutorial contains introductory and startup information, a section on each aspect of the program with sample applications, a separate section on macros, an index, and a pull-out booklet called "Quick Guide to Framework For Advanced Users of Spreadsheets." This booklet is written specifically for users of Lotus's 1-2-3, although others also may find it informative.

The reference manual is shorter than the tutorial. In addition to sections on each of the program applications, it features a brief chapter on printing, a long chapter on the FRED programming language, several appendices, a glossary, an index, and an alphabetically ordered list of commonly used Framework procedures with brief explanations.

As you learn Framework, you'll find that the manuals frequently provide complementary rather than identical information. If you can't find what you need in the tutorial, you might locate it in the reference manual. The package also includes an online tutorial, and context-sensitive help is available at any time during program operation.

Considering its power and scope, Framework uses only a moderate amount of memory—together, Framework and DOS take up only 170K. The entire package loads into your computer's working memory (RAM), including the database. Although the package supposedly requires 256K, it reportedly runs much faster in 384K, which is, in fact, required to run the telecommunications application.

Unlike the other integrated packages reviewed in this book, Framework's database capabilities dominate program operation. Unless you need a large matrix, however, the program's spreadsheet application should well satisfy your needs. Ashton-Tate has included a substantial array of functions, and if you need more, you may be able to use the FRED programming language to create your own.

InteCalc

COMPANY:	Schuchardt Software Systems
REQUIREMENTS:	PC-DOS; 128K; two disk drives.
LIMITS:	255 rows; 255 columns; 255 pages.
COMPATIBILITY:	InteMate, IntePert, IntePlan, InteWord; reads ASCII, DIF files.
PRICE:	$295

InteCalc is the spreadsheet component of the InteSoft Series, a "modular" series of programs that can operate alone or integrated with each other. The InteCalc spreadsheet has three distinguishing features. First, it's three dimensional, featuring "pages" as well as columns and rows. Second, InteCalc lets you display graphics characters anywhere on the screen. Third, the program has a user-interactive programming language, EXEC, that allows you to set up your own data input routines.

The added dimension of pages can best be explained by envisioning InteCalc as a spreadsheet "cube" measuring 255 rows by 255 columns by 255 pages. From the top, InteCalc's workspace looks like any other: a matrix of columns and rows. Rather than store spreadsheet models in separate files, however, the program "stacks" them one on top of the other like pages in a hardcopy report. Paging through the cube is accomplished with the Page Down and Page Up keys.

This added vertical axis lets you link sheets simply, quickly, and in a wide variety of ways. But InteCalc doesn't stop with simple sheet linkage. You can also "rotate" the cube for a "side view," allowing you to move vertically along a single row or column that cross-sections all pages. From this perspective, you can page horizontally through the cube, selecting, for example, a two-dimensional workspace that consists of all rows for column D. This kind of flexibility allows you to set up complex relationships among various data.

A sort capability compliments the cube construction, allowing you to sort on the basis of row, column, or page. Using this command to sort in descending numeric order for all three axes, for example, would bring the cell with the highest value to the top row of the first column of the first page.

InteCalc lets you display data in graphic form. Graphing, or "plotting," as the program's documentation calls it, is accomplished using the Title and Window commands, and must take place in a specially prepared cell. Like most good graphics applications, this one automatically changes graphs to reflect alterations in the data used to generate them. You can create graphs in any cell using any ASCII character.

The EXEC programming language, also used by Report Manager (reviewed later in this chapter), has been employed by InteCalc's programmers to create a number of interactive functions, including a template-building aid. Using procedures laid out in the manual, you can also employ EXEC to create functions not included in the program's built-in array. Best of all, you can use the simple statements that make up the EXEC language to set up your own automatic data entry routines.

Other than these three features, InteCalc provides fairly standard spreadsheet characteristics. It has numbered rows and lettered columns and pages. Each cell stores numbers, formulae, or text, and you can edit cell contents. Cell contents may be reproduced elsewhere in the report with or without relative changes to formulae. You can enter data through the keyboard, from other InteSoft programs, from ASCII or DIF data files, or through an EXEC program. A report can be stored in a form compatible with other InteSoft programs or in standard ASCII format.

You enter commands beginning with the slash key, followed by the string of letters appropriate to the specific command. The available options and sub-options appear along the bottom of the screen during every stage of command entry.

InteCalc has a set of built-in functions that include standard mathematical and trigonometric operations. You can implement conditional operations through InteCalc's macro programming facility. However, the program does not have logical operators in its command structure, and it's somewhat deficient in financial functions.

InteCalc's documentation is contained in a compact looseleaf notebook about 240 pages in length. It includes a lengthy and comprehensive tutorial, a command reference section, various appendices, a glossary, and an index. A reference card is also part of the package, and an online help facility is available during actual program operation. Help screens are context-sensitive and may be accessed from within the command procedure.

The InteCalc tutorial takes you through all of the basic command procedures by constructing sample worksheets. A helpful description of command syntax is provided in the introduction, and a novice could probably master the essential commands within a couple of days. The experienced spreadsheet user, with the help list and the reference card, will quickly become familiar with the program.

InteCalc handles errors relatively well. Error messages are displayed clearly onscreen, and are described in an appendix which also suggests corrective action. Since the command structure is straightforward, it's difficult to commit a serious error.

InteCalc has several flaws, among them being the lack of trained cursor movement, the absence of virtual memory, and primitive graphics compared to those found in integrated spreadsheet programs. However, good use of the EXEC language gives you the option to significantly expand available functions. You may find that InteCalc's three-dimensional format gives you not only great flexibility, but also an inclination to experiment with complex spreadsheet applications impossible with the more traditional, two-dimensional approach.

Open Access

COMPANY:	Software Products International
REQUIREMENTS:	PC-DOS, MS-DOS; 192K; two disk drives or hard disk.
LIMITS:	3,000 rows; 216 columns.
COMPATIBILITY:	Reads ASCII, DIF files.
PRICE:	$595

Open Access is an integrated package featuring six separate programs. Information Management, the primary component, is a database management system. The other programs are a spreadsheet, a word processor, a communications package, a graphics application, and a time manager.

The six programs come on two separate disks. Hard disk owners will be able to copy the contents of both disks onto their hard disk, but others will have to cope with disk swapping if they want to use the programs interactively. One disk contains the communications, word processing, and time management modules; the other contains information management, spreadsheet, and graphics.

The Open Access spreadsheet matrix is 216 columns by 3,000 rows. Most standard spreadsheet features are included. Numbers, formulae, or text may be entered into any cell, and long entries can spill over into adjacent cells. You control cursor movement with the arrow keys and the Page Up and Page Down keys, but there's no Goto command for jumping to a specified cell. Onscreen context-sensitive help is available at almost any point of program operation.

The spreadsheet is menu driven. Commands are initiated with the F2 key rather than the slash key. The program doesn't recalculate automatically, although it does handle forward referencing.

You can divide the screen into a maximum of six windows, specifying the size and location of each according to your needs. The windows can contain portions of up to four different spreadsheet reports. This feature is particularly valuable when you are creating a report that you want to link to an already existing one.

If you have a color monitor, the spreadsheet matrix appears in red and blue reverse video. The edit/entry line is pale blue—so pale, in fact, that it's almost impossible to see what you type during data entry. This flaw is a serious one; if your eyesight is not particularly good, you probably won't be able to see the characters at all.

The program features numerous special functions. Both conventional and modified Internal Rate of Return functions are included, and neither require that the investment cells be the initial row of the payments range. Additional functions are date and time, present and future value, depreciation, annuity, list, payment, table, and linear estimation.

The Open Access spreadsheet offers a feature called "Goal seeking," which is a What If...? capability in reverse. Instead of posing What If...? questions to determine the result of increased sales, for example, you can specify a desired goal and instruct the program to determine how much your sales have to increase in order to reach that goal.

Open Access documentation consists of a "Getting Started" booklet, a user's manual, and an "Information Management Reference Manual." The "Getting Started" booklet provides installation instructions for floppy disk and hard disk systems, a chapter on configuring your system for Open Access, printer information, and other more technical material. Installation is a long and sometimes difficult process. Instructions are poorly organized— in fact, one evaluator was unable install an Epson RX80 printer according to the directions.

The user's manual is divided into chapters on each program, plus a chapter titled "Integration and Macros," a glossary and listing of error messages, and an index. Unfortunately, the manual is printed in very small type with narrow margins, and the organization leaves much to be desired.

The spreadsheet section in the user's manual is not designed for beginners. Explanations are needlessly complex, and frequently incomplete (e.g., in a chapter called "Creating a New Model," the reader is not told how to enter the spreadsheet program). Although the section is intended to work as a tutorial, its organization is haphazard, and the authors assume the reader is already familiar with spreadsheet concepts and applications. A foldout page at the beginning of the spreadsheet section lists 27 commands with one-line descriptions. This is the extent of the command reference.

The index is actually six separate indexes, one for each of the six program chapters (except the "Integration & Macros" chapter). While the glossary is incomplete, the manual does include a listing of error messages and explanations. Error messages appear at the top of the screen, and many are self-explanatory.

Open Access doesn't provide a tutorial, so you must rely entirely on the user's manual to learn the program. Software Products International does, however, offer telephone support. In any case, previous experience with spreadsheets would be valuable.

To sum up, the Open Access spreadsheet offers most second-generation spreadsheet features. For those who use the program on a color monitor, however, the pale blue color of the edit/entry line will severely hamper ease of use. The lack of support from the documentation is another serious consideration. On the other hand, a substantial array of functions, sophisticated windowing, and especially the "Goal seeking" option, make Open Access a serious contender for a number of business needs.

Report Manager

COMPANY:	Datamension Corporation
REQUIREMENTS:	PC-DOS, MS-DOS; 128K; two disk drives or hard disk.
LIMITS:	255 rows, 255 columns, 255 pages.
COMPATIBILITY:	Project Manager, Records Manager, Task Manager; reads ASCII, DIF, SDI, SYLK files.
PRICE:	$495

The Advanced Version of Report Manager has several features that distinguish it from most other spreadsheets. To begin with, Report Manager is a three-dimensional program. Relying on what the program calls its "Datacube" configuration, Report Manager lets you create spreadsheets up to 255 rows by 255 columns, and "stack" these two-dimensional sheets up to 255 pages deep.

When using the program's Datacube ability, you can alter the screen display from the page mode, which shows rows and columns of a single page, to other modes. For example, the screen can display a single column of all rows and pages.

The second unusual feature of Report Manager is its graphics capability. Instead of settling for a single graphic character, graphs can take advantage of the computer's entire character set. After you establish the parameters for a given graph, it will immediately reflect any changes you make in the original figures. You can even place graphic borders around sections of a spreadsheet or its charts to dress up reports.

The third unique characteristic is the ability to generate your own automatic data entry routines using Report Manager's EXEC programming language. With this easy-to-use language, you can set up a file of commands that will prompt you to enter information, automatically assign values, and perform calculations in the sequence you designate. Setting up such automated models is a convenient way to tailor the program to specific applications, and can cut down on errors when someone unfamiliar with correct input procedure is running the program.

The program accepts values, text, or formulae into each cell. By using a three-stroke command, you can set up the program to move the cursor one cell right, left, up, or down after you input data, thereby saving time and keystrokes when entering data in long rows or columns. Report Manager is compatible with a monochrome monitor, but if you opt for a color graphics monitor, the program will make effective use of color to highlight different sections of the spreadsheet. The program accentuates cursor location, for example, by highlighting the appropriate cell coordinates on the spreadsheet's border.

Command options are displayed as full words and are initiated with the slash key. You can replicate a formula from one cell to another, and you can store and retrieve files at your discretion. Report Manager's sort utility permits you to arrange a series of cells in ascending or descending numeric or alphabetic order. You can store complex sort routines by entering the appropriate string of commands in a single cell; later, you can implement the routine simply by invoking the cell address. If you forget a command, a relatively complete online help function is accessible at any time.

Report Manager has a wealth of built-in functions. Financial functions include Internal Rate of Return, Present Value of a bond, as well as annuity and payment amount on a loan. Mathematical functions perform all standard trigonometric operations, and statistical functions include linear regression, modal value of a list, and standard deviation of a list. Each page may contain its own spreadsheet model.

The Report Manager user's manual is divided into two parts. The first part is an overview of basic program functions, including an explanation of the program's three-dimensionality, and its database, graphics, and user-programmable applications. The second part serves as a reference manual, and details editing, slash commands, and program customization. The index, glossary, and appendices are useful and comprehensive.

The manual's 12-page quick reference card offers very complete command definitions. As an added extra, a poster-sized flow chart delineates, in minute detail, Report Manager's command structure and hierarchy of functions. Unfortunately, the type on this chart is so small, its use as an easy reference tool is questionable.

Report Manager is both easy to learn and easy to operate. Moving to a cell on a different page requires that you enter a three- to five-character address, and the program clearly displays, in the lower right corner of the screen, the address of the cell where the cursor is located. You also can assign English names to as many as 100 different cells, and use these names in formulae rather than having to remember the cell address.

In general, Report Manager performs well, but it's missing some important features. First, the program's command structure does not permit an "If...then...else" statement in a formula. Nor do the formulae allow you to include the logical operators "and," "or," and "not." Second, while the graphic characters add a nice touch to the spreadsheet, they don't approach the capabilities of a true graphics application. In fact, such common configurations as line graphs and pie charts are out of the program's reach.

On the positive side, Report Manager includes features not found in some other packages. It reads and writes files in both DIF and ASCII formats, thereby allowing you to share data with many other programs. The EXEC facility gives you full programming capability, including the above mentioned "If...then...else" statement missing from normal program operation. Last but not least, the program's three-dimensional innovation lets you set up complex models impractical in a two-dimensional arena. If you need a powerful spreadsheet with unusual flexibility, Report Manager is definitely worth a try.

SuperCalc2

COMPANY:	Sorcim/IUS Micro Software
REQUIREMENTS:	PC-DOS, CP/M-80, CP/M-86; 64K; one disk drive.
LIMITS:	63 rows; 254 columns.
COMPATIBILITY:	SuperCalc; reads ASCII, DIF, SDI files.
PRICE:	$295

SuperCalc2, released in April 1983, includes all the features of the original SuperCalc, plus enough new commands, formatting options, and functions to qualify it as a second-generation spreadsheet program. Although the program publisher has since released SuperCalc3, a further upgrade incorporating integrated features (also reviewed in this chapter), SuperCalc2 holds its own in relation to other second-generation programs such as Multiplan.

Like its predecessor, SuperCalc2's matrix measures a relatively small 63 columns by 254 rows. The inclusion of variable column width, zero column width, title spillover, formula display, formula printout, split screen, and title locking also matches the original program's array of features.

New features include worksheet consolidation and keyboard macro facilities. SuperCalc2 also adds an Arrange command that allows you to sort text and numbers by row or column, in ascending or descending alphabetic or numeric order. A new Lookup data management function makes it easy to locate information in a table or chart.

SuperCalc2 maintains a very good selection of cell formatting options, adding a dollar sign format to the original SuperCalc list that includes handy formatting features like the zero as blank format (no display for cells containing zero), and scaling factor (used to automatically divide numbers by powers of 10). There is also a Hide command that allows you to suppress display and printout of specified cell contents.

Net Present Value is the only built-in financial function offered by SuperCalc2, but this sparseness is offset to some degree by a good selection of mathematical, trigonometric, and statistical functions, a full set of logical operations including "If...and" and "If...or" combinations, and date arithmetic. You can make date entries to cells and use references to those cells in computations, provided that the dates are between March 1, 1900 and February 28, 2100. Calendar functions include Date, Month, Day, Year, Today, Wday (Weekday), and Jdate. The Jdate function calculates a "Modified Julian Date," or a number ranging from 1 (for March 1, 1900) through 73,049 (for February 28, 2100).

SuperCalc2's documentation is complete, easy-to-use, and very well printed. A thorough installation guide is provided, along with a 20-page booklet, titled "10 Minutes to SuperCalc2," that takes the inexperienced user through startup procedures, and then explains how to build, edit, and print a simple spreadsheet report.

Another quick reference feature is the "SuperCalc2 Answer Card," designed for easy posting on a wall near your computer. A separate full-size

"Slash Commands Map," printed on stiff 3-hole punched paper, duplicates the slash command chart included on the Answer Card.

The SuperCalc2 user's manual is divided into a tutorial section and a reference section. There are five appendices and an index that lists symbols as well as commands, functions, and general terms. In addition, the manual includes a tutorial on SuperCalc2's data interchange system, Super-Data Interchange (SDI), and other reference material.

It's not hard to get started in SuperCalc2, since the comprehensive manual is supplemented by an online tutorial, supplying the first-time user with sample templates that clearly illustrate program capabilities. Commands are explained succinctly by context-sensitive help screens. Entering a command is easy, especially since the program provides an extensive array of user prompts.

SuperCalc2 has a high ease-of-use rating. The command structure is simple and it's easy to memorize keystroke patterns. Amenities such as the program's trained cursor control add to smoothness of operation. If you make a cell entry by pressing Enter, the cursor will move one cell in the same direction that it previously moved. This eliminates having to press an arrow key, unless you want to change direction—quite a time-saving feature for data entry personnel.

Errors in program operation generate such error messages as "Disk Full," "File Not Loadable," "Memory Full," and "Range Error," all of which appear at the bottom of the screen. The manual documents error messages and recommends corrective action. These recommendations are brief but complete in most cases (e.g., "The file name is not in proper format").

SuperCalc2 is compatible with programs that generate SDI-convertible files. As mentioned earlier, SDI is the utility provided with SuperCalc2 that converts data from one disk storage format to another. SDI files are virtually identical to VisiCalc's DIF files.

SuperCalc2 is an excellent value for its price. It's a sound, smoothly operating program with a lot of flexibility. Matching Multiplan in size and memory requirements, the program is short on financial functions, but offers date arithmetic and a strong selection of cell formatting features. In addition to its quality documentation, the detailed help screens and online tutorial make the program easy to learn. For those who prefer the slash key command structure over Multiplan's relatively complex command procedures, SuperCalc2 is certainly a good choice.

SuperCalc3

COMPANY:	Sorcim/IUS Micro Software
REQUIREMENTS:	PC-DOS; 96K; one disk drive or hard disk.
LIMITS:	9,999 rows; 127 columns.
COMPATIBILITY:	SuperCalc, SuperCalc2; reads ASCII, DIF, SDI files.
PRICE:	$395

SuperCalc3 incorporates significant advances over the general design and operational characteristics of its predecessors. The addition of graphics and database management capabilities improves its status considerably among other advanced spreadsheets. Release 2, the version evaluated in this review, has also enlarged the matrix to a whopping 9,999 rows by 127 columns, making it, as the program's promotional material states, "the largest usable spreadsheet."

Release 2 is also faster than earlier versions, and outstrips 1-2-3 in speed of calculation. Scrolling is quick and responsive; the End, Tab, Home, and Backtab keys move you rapidly to the limits of the workspace. In addition, the program highlights the cell coordinates on the display border that correspond to the current cursor location. Eight formats for cell contents are available.

Earlier versions of SuperCalc required that you place quotation marks around entries that you wanted represented as text. SuperCalc3 makes this requirement an option, and if you choose to do without the quotes, the program will automatically treat word entries as text unless they correspond to a cell address or built-in function. If you surround it with both parentheses and quotes, text can be integrated with formulae—a rare spreadsheet feature.

The program offers more than 200 command combinations and over 50 built-in financial, mathematical, trigonometrical, and textual functions. Financial functions include Internal Rate of Return, Level Payment, and Present and Future Value. SuperCalc3 also offers a random number generator, and several functions that allow you to write your own conditional logic statements. If you set the Global Calculation default to Iteration, Release 2 will automatically recalculate circular reference cells until they converge.

The sorting capabilities are similar to that of SuperCalc2, but SuperCalc3 also allows you to initiate a sort using only a primary and secondary key. The consolidation feature makes it possible to overlay different spreadsheet files, so that "stacked" cell values will combine to yield a single sum. Users who combine periodic reports having identical templates will find this type of consolidation particularly useful.

SuperCalc3's graphic capabilities rival that of many dedicated business graphics programs. You have eight graph types to choose from, and the option of medium- or high-resolution displays. Nine separate graphs can be constructed on a single spreadsheet. Once you've identified the appropriate cell range, pressing a single function key quickly generates the desired graph. Unlike many graphics applications "tacked on" to spreadsheets, this one creates perfectly round pie charts, clean lines, a variety of type fonts, and up to 99 colors. Eighteen plotters are supported, and you don't need a color monitor or graphics card to take advantage of the application.

The data management application, on the other hand, is somewhat primitive. Basically, it uses the spreadsheet itself to store as many as 9,998 records, with up to 127 fields per record, but you can only evaluate one row or column at a time. Entering the Arrange command gives you instant access to database records, and a single row serves as a field directory.

You can review material onscreen before you print it out, or you can save it on disk for later hardcopy output. Six type sizes and a variety of print formats are offered. As an added bonus, a program called "Sideways" allows you to print reports at a 90-degree angle. This means you can generate reports up to the maximum column width of the matrix without specifying ranges, then print them out, one by one, and paste them together later.

Context-sensitive help is available at any time. If you're in the middle of entering a command, pressing F1 calls up a color-coded Answer Screen that lists command options and relevant descriptions. SuperCalc3 also flags errors when they occur, and you can easily recover from errors without loss or damage to the spreadsheet. An appendix in the manual gives complete explanations of error messages and recommended corrective action.

The SuperCalc3 manual itself is divided into a user's guide (tutorial) and a reference section. The reference section describes the SuperCalc3 commands and functions. Two reference cards, one of commands and one of graphics options, are included in the package. A booklet describes the data interchange utility, and a brochure takes you through program basics.

A booklet entitled "10 Minutes to SuperCalc3" gives impatient users a quick tour of program features and functions. No online tutorial accompanies the manual, but sample data files help demonstrate simple to advanced spreadsheet applications.

SuperCalc3 installs easily, and no special procedures are required. The program is written in the "C" and assembly languages, so not only is it fast, it fits on a single disk. If you're looking for a spreadsheet with a wide array of options and great graphics, SuperCalc3 may be your best bet.

Symphony

COMPANY:	Lotus Development Corporation
REQUIREMENTS:	PC-DOS, MS-DOS; 320K; one disk drive or hard disk.
LIMITS:	8,192 rows; 256 columns.
COMPATIBILITY:	1-2-3, dBASE II (Ashton-Tate), VisiCalc (Software Arts); reads ASCII, DIF files.
PRICE:	$695

Symphony is the second major product published by Lotus Development Corporation. The first was 1-2-3, the innovative software package that combined spreadsheet, graphics, and database management capabilities in a single program. Symphony, an upgrade of 1-2-3, adds word processing and communications to the package, bringing the total number of applications to five.

The Symphony 256-column by 8,192-row spreadsheet is large, but its actual capacity will be determined by your computer's memory. Although you need a minimum of 320K RAM to run Symphony, the program itself takes up between 260-270K, and the entire worksheet is stored in memory. You may find that the 320K RAM minimum is really a bare minimum. One evaluator found that Symphony, like 1-2-3, does not reserve memory efficiently. For example, if you enter data in one section of the spreadsheet, then move to a distant group of cells and fill them with information, Symphony will reserve memory space for all of the blank cells that lie between the two sections.

All Symphony functions except graphics operate within the rows and columns of the spreadsheet. The macro capability, renamed the "command language" in Symphony, has been improved since 1-2-3. Symphony features more logical functions, including a number of string-manipulation functions. Password protection and hidden cells have been added. The Copy command has been upgraded to allow the duplication of the current value of a cell rather than its formula.

Symphony's unique windowing environment is the component that makes true integration of the program's various applications possible. Most users concur that Symphony's applications—except for the spreadsheet itself—work best when fully integrated, allowing you to share functions. To facilitate this, Symphony allows you to divide the screen into multiple windows, designate a particular application for each, and zoom in on a single window so that it fills the screen. Symphony lets you choose the dimensions and location of each window, and name it accordingly. You can choose either "tile" layout (which displays the windows next to each other), or "desktop" layout (which displays overlapping windows). Desktop layout lets you determine the extent of overlay. There's no limit to the number of windows you can create.

You can change a window to instantly reflect a different application. Your database can be transformed into a word processing document, for example, and your spreadsheet window into a communications window, at your command. You can include references to other windows in the window you're currently using, which allows you to incorporate information developed in a spreadsheet into a database.

Symphony's graphics application comes with certain limitations. If you're using a monochrome display adapter, your screen won't display graphics. If you're using a color adapter or Hercules board, you'll be able to view text and monochrome graphics simultaneously. If you're using a special-supported graphics board, your screen will display text and color graphs simultaneously. No matter what your equipment, Symphony isn't capable of printing text that is mixed with graphs.

Compared to many software packages, Symphony isn't the easiest to learn. It is generally recommended that beginners take it slowly, picking up one application at a time and waiting until they are familiar with each before using windows. Many evaluators agree that it takes a long time to master the program.

To help you out, an introductory level tutorial is provided on disk. Sixteen lessons are included, each 15 minutes long. Context-sensitive help screens are available at the touch of the F1 key.

Symphony's set of standard commands helps smooth the way when you switch from one application to another. There are 20 function key combinations, and a plastic overlay is included to remind you of each combination. The command language lets you store a series of commands for future use, making repetitive or complicated tasks easier to execute.

To sum up, Symphony is a remarkably powerful program, providing the capability to handle a number of important business tasks. Each of its component applications is acceptable, although only the spreadsheet can really hold its own against stand-alone programs. Symphony is also difficult to learn and use, and mastering it requires persistence and a great deal of time. This factor, together with its memory requirements and price tag, should be weighed against the program's advantages if you are considering the package for your own business use.

VisiCalc Package

COMPANY:	Software Arts, Inc.
REQUIREMENTS:	PC-DOS, MS-DOS; 64K (VisiCalc), 192K (Advanced Version); one disk drive (VisiCalc), two disk drives (Advanced Version).
LIMITS:	254 rows; 63 columns.
COMPATIBILITY:	Reads DIF files.
PRICE:	$179

The VisiCalc Package contains two separate spreadsheet programs. One is the original VisiCalc, the same popular spreadsheet that helped start the microcomputer revolution. The second half of the software package is called VisiCalc Advanced Version. This separate program uses the original VisiCalc structure, but adds a considerable number of new and useful financial, date, and time functions. Requiring three times the memory of the original, the Advanced Version also includes keyboard macros and a wealth of formatting functions.

In addition to holding the distinction as the first electronic spreadsheet designed for personal use, the original VisiCalc also sold more copies from 1979 to 1982 than any other business software product. It was also roundly imitated by many subsequent spreadsheet programs, and VisiCalc Advanced Version is hardly an exception. Row and column dimensions, cursor movement keys, and slash commands in the Advanced Version are virtually interchangeable with those found in the original.

The matrix measures 254 rows by 63 columns, and the program relies on the directional arrow keys to move the cursor from cell to cell. Hitting the greater than (>) key calls up a Goto prompt, at which point you can enter the address of the cell in which you want to enter or change data. The entry line, at the top of the screen, displays the address of the active cell and the type of data that cell contains.

The basic slash commands are easy to remember. For example, the command "/F" sets the stage for formatting an individual cell, and "/G" allows you to choose the global cell format for an entire matrix. You can set the global column width from three to 80 characters wide with the latter command. Unlike its earlier counterparts, the Advanced Version allows you to vary the width of individual columns as well. It also gives full-word prompts to help beginners learn command and data entry procedures.

VisiCalc Advanced Version boasts one of the most useful keyboard macro functions available. Rather than forcing you to go through a separate procedure, the program allows you to save a series of keystrokes as you execute them on the worksheet itself. You can store up to 26 command and data entry sequences, each one activated by a designated letter key. This straightforward facility can save you a considerable amount of time, especially if you often use the same command routines within different reports.

The Advanced Version probably offers more formatting options for numeric entries than any other spreadsheet, making it ideal for accounting applications. It also lets you make multiple copies of a single range of cells —a feature missing from most other programs. Date and time functions are also a step ahead of most of the competition, permitting you to calculate date and time intervals and convert fractions of a day into hours, minutes, and seconds.

Documentation for the VisiCalc Package is for both beginning and advanced users. To help you learn the basics, Software Arts has included a copy of Donald Beil's *The VisiCalc Book,* one of the many books written to explain the in's and out's of the original program. This well-written text exceeds the quality of most manuals, and takes you through the full array of program features without being too wordy or dependent on technical jargon.

The manual for the Advanced Version is sketchy, and relies heavily on an extensive but sometimes cryptic command reference card. Obviously, the publisher assumes that if you're familiar with the original VisiCalc, you won't need a comprehensive guide to the Advanced Version, since it uses the same command structure. All the same, the Advanced Version's new features and functions could be more comprehensively explained.

A user-interactive tutorial on disk covers both elementary and advanced features, and its well-designed lessons make up in part for the explanations of advanced features missing from the manual. VisiCalc Advanced Version's help system is both context-sensitive and available at any time during program operation. Online help was conspicuously absent in earlier versions, and comes as a welcomed addition. Software Arts has also included several ready-made spreadsheet templates.

The Advanced Version has built-in safeguards to ensure that you don't accidentally lose data. For instance, when you execute the Clear command, which erases the worksheet from memory and from the screen, you are prompted "Clear: type Y to confirm." Typing any other character cancels the command. You don't have to worry about losing files when you run out of room on a disk, because you can capture what's in computer memory by inserting any formatted disk when you receive the "Disk full" error message.

Installing the program is easy. Although both VisiCalc programs are copy protected, Software Arts provides an installation program to copy them onto a hard disk.

VisiCalc Advanced Version is a reliable and easy-to-use program. However, Software Arts left out many features which would have made it more competitive with other second-generation spreadsheets. No graphics functions or database management capabilities have been included, and there's no provision for title spillover or such important statistical functions as standard deviation and variance.

The VisiCalc Package's inclusion of both the original program and the Advanced Version may seem odd, but in the long run, it's a good value. Together both programs retail for less than almost any other spreadsheet, and you can always use the original version as a tutorial if you're interested primarily in the advanced program. While not as sophisticated as some of its counterparts, VisiCalc Advanced Version combines a straightforward command structure, a proven track record, and enough high-level functions to satisfy most spreadsheet users.

Chapter 6

Comparing Spreadsheet Products

This chapter contains a series of comprehensive tables that will allow you to compare, point by point, the spreadsheet software products reviewed throughout this book. The information found in these charts will provide you with the answers you'll need in order to complete the Needs Assessment Checklist in Chapter 3.

Full explanations of the various program features and functions are presented in earlier chapters. For fast and concise definitions, you may want to consult the Glossary or the Index.

- Table 6-1: Basic Information

- Table 6-2: Documentation

- Table 6-3: Screen Characteristics

- Table 6-4: Editing Functions

- Table 6-5: Cell Formatting

- Table 6-6: Print Formatting

- Table 6-6: File Handling

- Table 6-8: Recalculation

- Table 6-9: Mathematical & Trigonometric Functions

- Table 6-10: Financial & Statistical Functions

- Table 6-11: Logical & Specialized Functions

- Table 6-12: Integrated Features

TABLE 6-1: BASIC INFORMATION

PROGRAM	Price	Operating System	Program Written in	Minimum Memory (RAM)	Virtual Memory	Hard Disk Compatible	Copy Protected
AURA	$595	⁻PC-DOS, MS-DOS	C	256K	Yes	Yes	No
FRAMEWORK	$695	PC-DOS	Assembly	256K	No	Yes	Yes
INTECALC	$295	PC-DOS	Assembly	128K	Yes	Yes	No
MULTIPLAN	$195	PC-DOS, MS-DOS, CP/M	C	64K	No	Yes	No
1-2-3	$495	PC-DOS, MS-DOS	Assembly	192K	No	Yes	Yes
OPEN ACCESS	$695	PC-DOS, MS-DOS	Assembly	192K	Yes	Yes	No
REPORT MANAGER	$495	PC-DOS, MS-DOS	Assembly	192K	No	Yes	No
SUPERCALC 2	$295	PC-DOS, CP/M-80, CP/M-86	Assembly	64K	No	Yes	No
SUPERCALC 3	$395	PC-DOS	Assembly and C	128K	No	Yes	No
SYMPHONY	$695	PC-DOS, MS-DOS	Assembly	320K	Yes	Yes	No
VISICALC PACKAGE	$179*	PC-DOS, MS-DOS	Assembly	64K, 192K†	No	Yes	No

* Includes two spreadsheets: the original VisiCalc
  and VisiCalc Advanced Version.

† 64K for VisiCalc; 192K for Advanced Version.

‡ Toll-free number supplied to paid support subscribers.

TABLE 6-1 (Continued)

Demo Disk Available	Vendor Phone Support	Defective Disk Replacement		PROGRAM
No	512/328-5434‡	90-day guarantee		**AURA**
No	213/658-0086	90-day guarantee		**FRAMEWORK**
Yes	415/492-9330	90-day guarantee		**INTECALC**
No	206/828-8089	90-day guarantee		**MULTIPLAN**
No	617/253-9150	90-day guarantee		**1-2-3**
No	619/450-1526 800/321-1047	90-day guarantee		**OPEN ACCESS**
Yes	312/564-5060‡	90-day guarantee		**REPORT MANAGER**
No	408/942-0522	6-month guarantee		**SUPERCALC 2**
Yes	408/942-0522	6-month guarantee		**SUPERCALC 3**
No	617/253-9150	90-day guarantee		**SYMPHONY**
No	617/237-4000	90-day guarantee		**VISICALC PACKAGE**

TABLE 6-2: DOCUMENTATION

PROGRAM	MANUAL					OTHER AIDS			ONLINE HELP	
	Index	Tutorial	Glossary of Error Messages	Glossary of Terms	Tutorial on Disk	Sample Files on Disk	Quick Reference Card	Keyboard Templates	Always Available	Context Sensitive
AURA	Yes	Yes	Yes	Yes	Yes	Yes	Yes	Yes	Yes	Yes
FRAMEWORK	Yes	Yes	No	Yes	Yes	Yes	Yes	Yes	Yes	Yes
INTECALC	Yes	Yes	Yes	Yes	No	Yes	Yes	No	Yes	Yes
MULTIPLAN	No	Yes	Yes	Yes	No	Yes	Yes	No	Yes	Yes
1-2-3	Yes	Yes	Yes	Yes	Yes	Yes	Yes	No	Yes	Yes
OPEN ACCESS	Yes	Yes	Yes	Yes	Yes	Yes	Yes	Yes	Yes	No
REPORT MANAGER	Yes	Yes	Yes	Yes	Yes	Yes	Yes	Yes	Yes	No
SUPERCALC 2	Yes	Yes	Yes	Yes	Yes	Yes	Yes	No	Yes	Yes
SUPERCALC 3	Yes	Yes	Yes	Yes	Yes	Yes	Yes	No	Yes	Yes
SYMPHONY	Yes	Yes	No	Yes	Yes	Yes	Yes	Yes	Yes	Yes
VISICALC PACKAGE	Yes	Yes	Yes	No	No	No	No	No	Yes	Yes

TABLE 6-3: SCREEN CHARACTERISTICS

Rows	Columns	Windows	Jump to Chosen Cell	Title Locking	Title Spillover	Synchronous	Asynchronous	Page Dimension (3D)	PROGRAM
255	63	0	Yes	Has cell locking	Yes	Yes	Yes	No	AURA
30,000	30,000	*	No	Yes	Yes	No	No	No	FRAMEWORK
255	255	4	Yes	Yes	Yes	Yes	Yes	Yes	INTECALC
255	63	8	Yes	Yes	No	Yes	Yes	No	MULTIPLAN
2,048	230	2	Yes	Yes	Yes	Yes	Yes	N/A	1-2-3
3,000	216	6	Yes	Yes	Yes	No	Yes	Yes	OPEN ACCESS
255	255	4	Yes	Yes	No	Yes	Yes	Yes	REPORT MANAGER
63	254	2	Yes	Yes	Yes	Yes	Yes	No	SUPERCALC 2
9,999	127	2	Yes	Yes	Yes	Yes	Yes	No	SUPERCALC 3
8,192	256	5	Yes	Yes	Yes	Yes	Yes	No	SYMPHONY
254	63	2	Yes	Yes	No	Yes	Yes	No	VISICALC PACKAGE

* Limited by RAM only.

TABLE 6-3 (Continued)

PROGRAM	SCREEN DISPLAYS							ENTRY AIDS	
	Memory Status	Current Filename	Caps Lock Indicator	Num Lock Indicator	Color Highlighting	Hides Coordinates	User Prompts	Forms Mode	
AURA	Yes	Yes	No	No	No	No	Yes	No	
FRAMEWORK	No	Yes	Yes	Yes	No	No	Yes	No	
INTECALC	Yes	Yes	Yes	Yes	Yes	Yes	Yes	Yes	
MULTIPLAN	Yes	Yes	No	No	Yes	No	Yes	No	
1-2-3	Yes	Yes	Yes	Yes	No	Yes	Yes	Yes	
OPEN ACCESS	Yes	Yes	No	No	Yes	Yes	Yes	Yes	
REPORT MANAGER	Yes	Yes	Yes	Yes	Yes	Yes	Yes	Yes	
SUPERCALC 2	Yes	No	No	No	Yes	Yes	Yes	No	
SUPERCALC 3	Yes	No	Yes	Yes	Yes	Yes	Yes	No	
SYMPHONY	No	No	Yes	Yes	Yes	No	No	No	
VISICALC PACKAGE	Yes	No	No	No	No	No	No	Yes	

TABLE 6-4: EDITING FUNCTIONS

Edit Cell Contents	Set Cursor Direction	Erase Range of Cells	Move/Copy Range of Cells	Replicate Function	Copy Cell Format	Delete Column/Row	Insert Column/Row	Clear Report	Tab Search Function	Global Search and Replace	PROGRAM
Yes	Yes	Yes	Yes	Yes	Yes	Yes	Yes	Yes	Yes	Yes	AURA
Yes	No	Yes	Yes	Yes	Yes	Yes	Yes	Yes	No	Yes	FRAMEWORK
Yes	Yes	Yes	Yes	Yes	Yes	Yes	Yes	Yes	Yes	No	INTECALC
Yes	No	Yes	Yes	Yes	Yes	Yes	Yes	No	No	No	MULTIPLAN
Yes	Yes	Yes	Yes	Yes	Yes	Yes	Yes	Yes	No	No	1-2-3
Yes	Yes	Yes	Yes	Yes	Yes	Yes	Yes	Yes	Yes	Yes	OPEN ACCESS
Yes	Yes	Yes	Yes	Yes	Yes	Yes	Yes	Yes	Yes	No	REPORT MANAGER
Yes	Yes	Yes	Yes	Yes	No	Yes	Yes	Yes	No	No	SUPERCALC 2
Yes	Yes	Yes	Yes	Yes	No	Yes	Yes	Yes	Yes	No	SUPERCALC 3
Yes	Yes	Yes	Yes	Yes	Yes	Yes	Yes	Yes	No	No	SYMPHONY
Yes	Yes	Yes	Yes	Yes	Yes	Yes	Yes	Yes	No	No	VISICALC PACKAGE

TABLE 6-4 (Continued)

PROGRAM	English Cell Names	English Range Names
AURA	Yes	Yes
FRAMEWORK	Yes	No
INTECALC	Yes	No
MULTIPLAN	No	No
1-2-3	Yes	Yes
OPEN ACCESS	Yes	Yes
REPORT MANAGER	Yes	No
SUPERCALC 2	No	No
SUPERCALC 3	No	No
SYMPHONY	Yes	Yes
VISICALC PACKAGE	No	No

TABLE 6-5: CELL FORMATTING

Automatic Commas	Dollars & Cents	Credit/Debit Notation	Parentheses for Negative	Aligns by Decimal Point	Mixed Cells	Cell Protection	TEXT JUSTIFICATION			PROGRAM
							Right	Left	Center	
Yes	Yes	No	Yes	Yes	Yes	Yes	Yes	Yes	Yes	AURA
Yes	Yes	No	Yes	Yes	No	Yes	Yes	Yes	Yes	FRAMEWORK
Yes	Yes	Yes	Yes	No	Yes	No	Yes	Yes	No	INTECALC
Yes	Yes	No	No	No	No	Yes	Yes	Yes	Yes	MULTIPLAN
Yes	Yes	No	Yes	Yes	Yes	Yes	Yes	Yes	Yes	1-2-3
Yes	Yes	Yes	Yes	Yes	Yes	Yes	Yes	Yes	Yes	OPEN ACCESS
Yes	Yes	Yes	Yes	No	No	No	Yes	Yes	No	REPORT MANAGER
Yes	Yes	No	Yes	Yes	Yes	Yes	Yes	Yes	No	SUPERCALC 2
Yes	Yes	No	Yes	Yes	Yes	Yes	Yes	Yes	Yes	SUPERCALC 3
Yes	Yes	No	Yes	No	No	Yes	Yes	Yes	No	SYMPHONY
No	No	Yes	Yes	Yes	No	Yes	Yes	Yes	Yes	VISICALC PACKAGE

TABLE 6-5 (Continued)

PROGRAM	NUMBER JUSTIFICATION			CENTER TITLES		ADJUST WIDTH		
	Right	Left	Center	Horizontally	Vertically	Individually	Globally	Graphics Format
AURA	Yes	Yes	Yes	No	No	Yes	No	Yes
FRAMEWORK	Yes	Yes	No	No	No	Yes	Yes	No
INTECALC	Yes	Yes	No	Yes	Yes	Yes	Yes	Yes
MULTIPLAN	Yes	Yes	Yes	No	No	Yes	Yes	Yes
1-2-3	Yes	No	No	No	No	Yes	Yes	Yes
OPEN ACCESS	Yes	Yes	Yes	Yes	Yes	Yes	Yes	Yes
REPORT MANAGER	Yes	Yes	No	Yes	Yes	Yes	Yes	Yes
SUPERCALC 2	Yes	Yes	No	No	No	Yes	Yes	Yes
SUPERCALC 3	Yes	Yes	No	No	No	Yes	Yes	Yes
SYMPHONY	No	No	No	No	No	Yes	Yes	Yes
VISICALC PACKAGE	Yes	Yes	Yes	No	No	Yes	Yes	Yes

TABLE 6-5   (Continued)

Adjust Row Height	Display Formulae in Cells	Hide Cell Contents	Percent Format for Decimals	Scientific Notation	Two Decimal	Fixed Decimal	Integer Format	Global Formatting Options	PROGRAM
No	Yes	Yes	Yes	Yes	Yes	No	No	Yes	AURA
No	No	No	Yes	Yes	Yes	Yes	Yes	Yes	FRAMEWORK
No	Yes	No	No	Yes	Yes	Yes	Yes	Yes	INTECALC
No	Yes	Yes	Yes	Yes	Yes	Yes	Yes	Yes	MULTIPLAN
No	Yes	No	Yes	Yes	Yes	Yes	Yes	Yes	1-2-3
No	Yes	Yes	Yes	Yes	No	Yes	Yes	Yes	OPEN ACCESS
No	Yes	No	No	Yes	Yes	Yes	Yes	Yes	REPORT MANAGER
No	Yes	Yes	Yes	Yes	Yes	No	Yes	Yes	SUPERCALC 2
No	Yes	Yes	Yes	Yes	Yes	No	Yes	Yes	SUPERCALC 3
No	Yes	Yes	Yes	Yes	Yes	Yes	Yes	Yes	SYMPHONY
No	Yes	Yes	Yes	Yes	Yes	Yes	Yes	Yes	VISICALC PACKAGE

TABLE 6-6: PRINT FORMATTING

PROGRAM	Printer Installation	Printer Setup Strings	Select Control Codes	Graphics Output	Use Alternate Font	Print Formulae	Print Screen Contents	Print Partial Report	Print Report in Pages	Fit Output to Paper	Report Generator
AURA	No	Yes	Yes	Yes	Yes	Yes	Yes	Yes	Yes	Yes	No
FRAMEWORK	Yes	Yes	No	Yes	Yes	No	Yes	No	Yes	Yes	No
INTECALC	No	Yes	Yes	Yes	No	Yes	Yes	Yes	Yes	No	No
MULTIPLAN	No	Yes	Yes	Yes	Yes	Yes	Yes	No	Yes	Yes	No
1-2-3	Yes	Yes	Yes	Yes	No	Yes	Yes	Yes	Yes	Yes	No
OPEN ACCESS	Yes	Yes	Yes	Yes	No	Yes	Yes	Yes	Yes	Yes	Yes
REPORT MANAGER	Yes	Yes	Yes	Yes	Yes	Yes	Yes	Yes	Yes	No	Yes
SUPERCALC 2	No	Yes	Yes	No	No	Yes	Yes	Yes	No	Yes	No
SUPERCALC 3	Yes	Yes	Yes	Yes	Yes	Yes	Yes	Yes	No	Yes	No
SYMPHONY	Yes	Yes	Yes	Yes	No	Yes	Yes	Yes	Yes	Yes	No
VISICALC PACKAGE	No	Yes	Yes	No	Yes	Yes	Yes	Yes	Yes	Yes	No

TABLE 6-7: FILE HANDLING

Specify Logged Drive	Read Partial Report	Save Partial Report	Copy File Command	Delete File Command	Rename File Command	ASCII Files	DIF Files	SDI Files	SYLK Files	Merge Files Command	PROGRAM
						READS					
No	Yes	No	Yes	Yes	Yes	Yes	No	No	No	No	AURA
Yes	No	No	No	Yes	No	Yes	No	No	No	Yes	FRAMEWORK
Yes	No	No	Yes	Yes	No	Yes	Yes	No	No	Yes	INTECALC
Yes	No	No	No	Yes	Yes	No	No	No	Yes	No	MULTIPLAN
No	No	Yes	Yes	Yes	Yes	Yes	Yes	No	No	No	1-2-3
Yes	No	Yes	Yes	Yes	Yes	Yes	Yes	No	No	Yes	OPEN ACCESS
Yes	No	No	No	Yes	No	Yes	Yes	Yes	Yes	No	REPORT MANAGER
Yes	Yes	Yes	No	No	No	Yes	Yes	Yes	No	No	SUPERCALC 2
Yes	Yes	Yes	No	No	No	Yes	Yes	Yes	No	No	SUPERCALC 3
Yes	No	Yes	Yes	Yes	No	Yes	Yes	No	No	No	SYMPHONY
Yes	No	No	No	Yes	No	No	Yes	No	No	No	VISICALC PACKAGE

TABLE 6-7 (Continued)

PROGRAM	Consolidate Report	Link Individual Cells	Link Separate Reports	
AURA	Yes	Yes	Yes	
FRAMEWORK	Yes	Yes	Yes	
INTECALC	Yes	Yes	No	
MULTIPLAN	No	Yes	Yes	
1-2-3	No	Yes	No	
OPEN ACCESS	Yes	Yes	Yes	
REPORT MANAGER	Yes	Yes	Yes	
SUPERCALC 2	Yes	No	No	
SUPERCALC 3	Yes	No	No	
SYMPHONY	Yes	Yes	No	
VISICALC PACKAGE	Yes	Yes	No	

TABLE 6-8: RECALCULATION

Manual Option	Recalculate by Column	Recalculate by Row	Natural Recalculation	Recalculate Upon Loading		PROGRAM
Yes	No	No	Yes	Yes		AURA
Yes	Yes	Yes	Yes	No		FRAMEWORK
Yes	No	No	Yes	No		INTECALC
Yes	No	No	No	Yes		MULTIPLAN
Yes	Yes	Yes	Yes	Yes		1-2-3
Yes	Yes	Yes	Yes	No		OPEN ACCESS
Yes	No	No	Yes	Yes		REPORT MANAGER
Yes	Yes	Yes	Yes	Yes		SUPERCALC 2
Yes	Yes	Yes	Yes	Yes		SUPERCALC 3
Yes	Yes	Yes	Yes	No		SYMPHONY
Yes	Yes	Yes	No	Yes		VISICALC PACKAGE

TABLE 6-9:
MATHEMATICAL & TRIGONOMETRIC FUNCTIONS

PROGRAM	Raise to a Power	Square Root	Sign of Value	Modulo	Logarithm	Tangent	Cosine	Sine	Arc Tangent	Arc Cosine	Arc Sine
AURA	No	Yes	Yes	Yes	Yes	Yes	Yes	Yes	Yes	Yes	Yes
FRAMEWORK	Yes	Yes	Yes	Yes	Yes	Yes	Yes	Yes	Yes	Yes	Yes
INTECALC	Yes	Yes	No	Yes	Yes	Yes	Yes	Yes	Yes	Yes	Yes
MULTIPLAN	Yes	Yes	Yes	No	Yes	Yes	Yes	Yes	Yes	Yes	Yes
1-2-3	Yes	Yes	No	Yes	Yes	Yes	Yes	Yes	Yes	Yes	Yes
OPEN ACCESS	Yes	Yes	No	Yes	Yes	Yes	Yes	Yes	Yes	Yes	Yes
REPORT MANAGER	Yes	Yes	Yes	Yes	Yes	Yes	Yes	Yes	Yes	Yes	Yes
SUPERCALC 2	Yes	Yes	Yes	Yes	Yes	Yes	Yes	Yes	Yes	Yes	Yes
SUPERCALC 3	Yes	Yes	Yes	Yes	Yes	Yes	Yes	Yes	Yes	Yes	Yes
SYMPHONY	Yes	Yes	No	Yes	Yes	Yes	Yes	Yes	Yes	Yes	Yes
VISICALC PACKAGE	Yes	Yes	Yes	Yes	No	Yes	Yes	Yes	Yes	Yes	Yes

TABLE 6-9 (Continued)

Radian/Degree Conversion	Pi	Sum of a List	Integer Value	Rounded Value	Absolute Value	Random Value	PROGRAM
No	Yes	Yes	Yes	Yes	Yes	No	AURA
Yes	Yes	Yes	Yes	Yes	Yes	Yes	FRAMEWORK
Yes	No	Yes	Yes	No	Yes	Yes	INTECALC
No	Yes	Yes	Yes	Yes	Yes	No	MULTIPLAN
No	Yes	Yes	Yes	Yes	Yes	No	1-2-3
No	No	Yes	Yes	Yes	Yes	No	OPEN ACCESS
Yes	No	Yes	Yes	Yes	Yes	Yes	REPORT MANAGER
No	Yes	Yes	Yes	Yes	Yes	Yes	SUPERCALC 2
Yes	Yes	Yes	Yes	Yes	Yes	Yes	SUPERCALC 3
Yes	Yes	Yes	Yes	Yes	Yes	Yes	SYMPHONY
No	Yes	Yes	Yes	Yes	Yes	No	VISiCALC PACKAGE

TABLE 6-10: FINANCIAL & STATISTICAL FUNCTIONS

PROGRAM	Annuity	Interest on Loan	Average Value in List	Maximum Value in List	Minimum Value in List	Count Items in List	Future Value	Net Present Value	Internal Rate of Return	Payment	Depreciation
AURA	Yes	Yes	Yes	Yes	No	No	No	Yes	Yes	Yes	Yes
FRAMEWORK	Yes	Yes	Yes	Yes	No	No	No	Yes	Yes	Yes	Yes
INTECALC	Yes	Yes	Yes	Yes	Yes	Yes	Yes	Yes	Yes	Yes	Yes
MULTIPLAN	Yes	Yes	Yes	Yes	No	No	Yes	Yes	Yes	Yes	Yes
1-2-3	Yes	Yes	Yes	Yes	Yes	No	Yes	Yes	Yes	Yes	Yes
OPEN ACCESS	Yes	Yes	Yes	Yes	Yes	Yes	Yes	Yes	Yes	Yes	Yes
REPORT MANAGER	Yes	Yes	Yes	Yes	Yes	Yes	Yes	Yes	Yes	Yes	Yes
SUPERCALC 2	Yes	Yes	Yes	Yes	No	No	No	Yes	Yes	Yes	Yes
SUPERCALC 3	Yes	Yes	Yes	Yes	No	No	No	Yes	Yes	Yes	Yes
SYMPHONY	Yes	Yes	Yes	Yes	No	No	No	Yes	Yes	Yes	Yes
VISICALC PACKAGE	Yes	Yes	Yes	Yes	No	No	No	Yes	Yes	Yes	Yes

TABLE 6-10   (Continued)

Modal Value	Sum of Squares	Standard Deviation	Regression Analysis	Variance	Other Functions	PROGRAM
No	No	Yes	No	Yes	No	**AURA**
No	No	Yes	No	Yes	MIRR*	**FRAMEWORK**
Yes	Yes	Yes	Yes	No	Amortization	**INTECALC**
No	No	Yes	No	No	No	**MULTIPLAN**
Yes	No	Yes	Yes	Yes	No	**1-2-3**
No	No	Yes	Yes	Yes	MIRR,* DEPR, and NOT (X)	**OPEN ACCESS**
Yes	Yes	Yes	Yes	No	Amortization, loan payment, no. of payments, present value, annuity due/bond	**REPORT MANAGER**
Yes	No	No	No	No	No	**SUPERCALC 2**
Yes	No	No	No	No	No	**SUPERCALC 3**
No	No	Yes	No	Yes	Yes	**SYMPHONY**
No	No	No	No	No	Natural exponent	**VISICALC PACKAGE**

* Modified Internal Rate of Return

TABLE 6-11: LOGICAL & SPECIALIZED FUNCTIONS

PROGRAM	Alphabetic Sorting	Numeric Sorting	Choose	Lookup	And	Or	Not	Nested Conditionals	If...Then	If...Then ...Else
AURA	Yes	Yes	Yes	Yes	Yes	Yes	Yes	No	Yes	No
FRAMEWORK	Yes	Yes	Yes	Yes	Yes	Yes	Yes	Yes	Yes	Yes
INTECALC	Yes	Yes	No	Yes	Yes	Yes	Yes	Yes	Yes	No
MULTIPLAN	Yes	Yes	No	Yes	Yes	Yes	Yes	Yes	No	Yes
1-2-3	Yes	Yes	Yes	Yes	Yes	Yes	Yes	Yes	Yes	Yes
OPEN ACCESS	Yes	Yes	Yes	Yes	Yes	Yes	Yes	Yes	Yes	Yes
REPORT MANAGER	Yes	Yes	No	Yes	Yes	Yes	Yes	Yes	Yes	Yes
SUPERCALC 2	Yes	Yes	No	Yes	Yes	Yes	Yes	Yes	Yes	Yes
SUPERCALC 3	Yes	Yes	No	Yes	Yes	Yes	Yes	Yes	Yes	Yes
SYMPHONY	Yes	Yes	Yes	Yes	Yes	Yes	Yes	Yes	No	Yes
VISICALC PACKAGE	No	No	Yes	Yes	Yes	Yes	Yes	Yes	Yes	Yes

The header spanning "LOGICAL OPERATORS" covers the columns: And, Or, Not, Nested Conditionals, If...Then, If...Then...Else

TABLE 6-11   (Continued)

Date Entries	Time Entries	Today's Date	Time of Day	Day of Week	Date Intervals	Time Intervals	PROGRAM
			DISPLAYS		CALCULATES		
Yes	No	Yes	Yes	No	Yes	No	AURA
Yes	Yes	No	No	Yes	No	No	FRAMEWORK
Yes	Yes	Yes	Yes	Yes	Yes	Yes	INTECALC
No	No	No	No	No	No	No	MULTIPLAN
Yes	No	Yes	No	Yes	Yes	Yes	1-2-3
Yes	No	Yes	Yes	No	No	Yes	OPEN ACCESS
Yes	Yes	Yes	Yes	Yes	Yes	Yes	REPORT MANAGER
Yes	No	Yes	No	Yes	No	No	SUPERCALC 2
Yes	No	Yes	No	Yes	No	No	SUPERCALC 3
Yes	Yes	Yes	Yes	Yes	No	No	SYMPHONY
Yes	Yes	No	No	No	Yes	Yes	VISICALC PACKAGE

TABLE 6-12: INTEGRATED FUNCTIONS

PROGRAM	Built-in Graphics	Built-in Word Processing	Built-in Database Management	Built-in Data Communications	Keystroke Macros	Internal Programming Language
AURA	Yes	Yes	Yes	No	Yes	No
FRAMEWORK	Yes	Yes	Yes	Yes	Yes	Yes
INTECALC	Yes	Yes	Yes	No	No	Yes
MULTIPLAN	No	No	No	No	No	No
1-2-3	Yes	No	Yes	No	Yes	No
OPEN ACCESS	Yes	Yes	Yes	Yes	Yes	No
REPORT MANAGER	No	No	No	No	Yes	Yes
SUPERCALC 2	Yes	No	No	No	No	No
SUPERCALC 3	Yes	No	Yes	No	No	Yes
SYMPHONY	Yes	Yes	Yes	Yes	Yes	Yes
VISICALC PACKAGE	Yes	No	Yes	No	Yes	No

Part III

Electronic Spreadsheet Resources

Glossary

General Computer Terms

Application software A computer program designed to perform a specific task or function, e.g., word processing, data base management, financial analysis, spreadsheet, etc.

ASCII Acronym for American Standard Code for Information Interchange. A standardized format for encoding characters and functions used by computers. Many word processing programs, for example, read text and data in ASCII format so that they can exchange files with other programs.

Asynchronous communications adapter Used to connect a modem to a computer. This device does not need special timing signals from the computer or host to transfer data. See communications card.

Backup A reserve copy of information in computer memory, retained on tape or disk in the event the original is lost or damaged.

BASIC Acronym for Beginner's All-purpose Symbolic Instruction Code. A high-level computer programming language originally developed at Dartmouth College as an instructional tool. BASIC is the most common language available for microcomputers.

Baud The speed or rate of computer data flow.

Benchmark An historically significant software program that represents a standard against which other programs of the same type or application are measured. Although it may have been a best-seller at one time, a benchmark program may no longer be the "best" in its software category.

Bit Derived from the words "binary digit," this is the most elementary form of data used by a computer. Each bit has a value of either one or zero (1 or 0); a string of eight bits makes one byte.

Boolean operators The logical operators "and," "or," "not," "except," "if," "then," and "else" used separately or in various combinations by a computer program to decide if a statement is true or false or to assist in the retrieval of specific information based on these values; named after the English mathematician, George Boole.

Boot A general term used to describe starting up a microcomputer system.

Byte A single character of data used by a computer. Each byte is comprised of eight bits.

Central processing unit (CPU) Like a switchboard, the main body of a computer where data is controlled (i.e., routed and processed) by means of a system of internal microprocessors.

Character A single letter, number, or symbol representing a byte of binary data. A character can also be a space, tab, or carriage return.

Command A sequence of keystrokes that activates a particular program function.

Communications card Also referred to as a communications adaptor. A plug-in board often required by a central processing unit in order to facilitate the interface between a computer and a modem.

Configure To setup a computer system for a specific purpose, such as compatibility with certain hardware and/or software.

CP/M Acronym for Control Program for Microprocessors. A computer operating system created by Digital Research Corporation for microcomputers with 8-bit CPUs.

CP/M-86 An operating system created by Digital Research Corporation for microcomputers with 16-bit CPUs.

CRT Acronym for cathode ray tube; the picture tube used in a computer display unit.

Cursor An electronic position marker on the video display screen. Cursor location and function is controlled through keyboard or mouse commands.

Data The actual information stored in a field.

Database A structured collection of related information stored in one or more files and serving one or more applications. The database is independent from and should not be confused with the program that actually manipulates the information.

Data disk A blank disk formatted for your computer operating system and used to store your program records. For example, these disks may contain all of your business's accounting records or word processing documents.

Data Interchange Format (DIF) A format for data files that allows the data to be accessed by more than one type of program. DIF was designed to format data for transfer from one program to another by Software Arts, Inc.

Default Refers to a value or an instruction that is automatically accepted by a computer program unless the current operator enters a different instruction.

Disk A general term referring to either a floppy disk or a hard disk. A floppy disk is a flexible magnetic recording medium housed inside a plastic envelope. A hard disk is not flexible or removable, and is housed inside a closed case. Hard disks have a greater storage capacity than floppy disks.

Disk drive A computer memory device that allows fast and accurate positioning within and between data files, operating instructions, and portable and fixed storage media. Disk drives allow entry, updating, and changing of data through read/write operations.

Disk emulator See RAM disk.

Disk operating system (DOS) A collection of programs that controls input, output, and internal management of data in a computer and on disk.

Documentation Instructional material, primarily in written form, that explains the operation of specific software or hardware.

Dot matrix printer A printer that produces characters made up of arrays of dots. These printers are faster and less expensive than letter quality printers.

Double density A disk drive system that keeps twice as much information in the same space as a single-density system. Also used to refer to a disk that has information stored on it via a double-density disk drive system.

Double sided A disk drive system in which information can be stored and extracted from both sides of a disk. If, for instance, a single-sided, single-density, 5 1/4-inch disk can hold 90,000 bytes of information (90K), then a double-sided or a double-density disk would hold 180K, and a double-sided, double-density disk would hold 360K.

Download Move information from a central host computer to a smaller unit.

8-bit microprocessor A microprocessor that moves information through the computer in groups of eight bits.

Electronic disk See RAM disk.

Encode The process of electromagnetically writing information onto the magnetic surface of a disk or tape.

Error message A screen indication that a particular error has occurred. For example, "Warning: Disk Full" would indicate that the memory limit has been exceeded.

Error recovery The methods made available by a software program for remedying errors. An irrecoverable error is one that forces loss of data or exit from the program.

External memory Refers to mass storage devices, the most common of which is a magnetic disk drive.

Field An area in a record stored in computer memory which is set aside for a specific type of information.

File A collection of specific information, usually consisting of records, that is stored in a logical fashion.

Floppy disk See disk.

Format To prepare a disk for storing data.

Function key A key that has a special function controlled by the program. Function keys often provide the convenience of pressing one key instead of a series of keys.

Hardcopy Output printed on paper by a computer.

Hard disk A nonremovable data disk sealed inside the computer cabinet; also known as a fixed disk. A hard disk provides large amounts of storage (typically, 10 megabytes) and rapid access.

Hardware The physical components of a computer system, e.g., monitor, keyboard, printer, CPU, etc.

Head A small electromagnet used to read or write information onto the magnetic surface of a tape, disk, or drum.

Input Information that is entered into a computer system.

Integrated software Computer software that contains several application programs in a single package; designed to allow easy exchange of information between the constituent programs.

Interface A connection or common boundary enabling a system or program to acquire information from another system or program; also describes interaction between user and computer.

Kilobyte Abbreviated "K," a kilobyte equals 1,024 bytes of memory.

Justification The adjustment or spacing of character lines to a uniform length at margins.

Letter quality printer A printer that produces characters made up of letter quality letters. These printers are slower and more expensive than dot matrix printers.

Megabyte Abbreviated "M," a megabyte consists of 1,024K or approximately one million bytes of memory.

Memory The data storage areas in a computer. Data stored on microchip is in random access memory (RAM), and is emptied when the computer is turned off. Data stored on tape or on disk is in read only memory (ROM), and remains intact when the computer is turned off.

Menu A screen display listing the commands, options, or selections currently available for execution.

Microchip Also called a chip, a small piece of silicon or other semiconductor that has been etched with a microscopic pattern of circuits. Chips are the building blocks of computer memory.

Microcomputer A small but complete microprocessor-based computer system that can be used by one person at a time.

Microprocessor The microchip that contains a microcomputer's central data processing circuitry.

Mode A condition or status of a program that usually implies readiness to perform a certain kind of task, such as an "editing mode."

Modem A communication device that permits the transfer of data between computers over standard telephone lines.

MS-DOS A disk operating system designed by Microsoft, Inc. MS-DOS ("MS" for Microsoft) is the software's generic name, while PC-DOS is the specific implementation of MS-DOS for the IBM PC.

Multiuser A computer system that can be used by more than one person at the same time.

Operating system The program that controls the most basic operations of the computer. The operating system interfaces application software with computer hardware.

Output Information sent by the computer to a screen, printer, plotter, or storage device.

Parallel port Allows eight bits of data to be transferred back and forth between the computer and a peripheral device such as a printer.

PC-DOS An operating system that is the specific implementation of MS-DOS for the IBM PC.

Peripherals Additional hardware that is connected to the basic computer (e.g., printer, modem, joystick).

Plotter A computer output device that draws figures, diagrams, or other graphics using one or more colored pens.

Port A point in a computer's circuitry designed for data input or output. A printer is connected to a computer via either a parallel or a serial port.

Printer A computer output device that prints characters or graphics on paper.

Program A set of computer instructions, also known as software.

Prompt A symbol or statement that appears onscreen to indicate that a program, a language, or an operating system is ready for use.

RAM disk An electronic disk created with extra Random Access Memory.

Random access A mode of data access where data or blocks of data can be read directly, and in any order. This makes it unnecessary to read all the way from the beginning of a file or block of data to obtain the desired information.

Random access memory (RAM) Memory that allows the user direct access to any storage location; information can be written into or read out of these locations. Also called user memory, RAM is volatile; its contents are lost when power is turned off.

Read-only memory (ROM) Memory in which data is stored permanently. Such memory is nonvolatile, as it is unaffected when power is turned off.

Read/write head See Head.

RS-232 A standard for connecting data processing and data communications hardware (i.e., computers, terminals, printers, plotters, modems, etc.) with serial interfaces, established by the Electronic Industries Association in 1969.

Screen Same as CRT, video display, or monitor.

Serial port Transfers one bit of data back and forth between the computer and a peripheral device such as a printer.

Single density A disk drive system that has a space capacity, which is half as much as a double-density disk drive system, in the same amount of space.

Single sided A disk drive system that only reads or writes data on one side of a disk, as compared with double-sided disk drives.

16-bit microprocessor A microprocessor that moves information through the computer in groups of 16 bits.

Smart modem A modem that is controlled by the user from the computer instead of through switches on the modem itself.

Software Information and instructions that direct computers to perform specified tasks, as opposed to the electronic devices (hardware) which execute them. All computer programs are software.

UCSD p-System A disk operating system that operates as a kind of universal translator. The p-System was developed by the University of California at San Diego (UCSD) and is usually packaged with one or more programming languages.

Utilities Programs that perform routine operations, e.g., data integrity checks or file sharing.

Spreadsheet Software Terms

Active cell The spreadsheet cell containing the cursor. The active cell is the cell that receives the current entry.

Address A reference to a particular spreadsheet cell. For example, A15 is the address of the cell at the intersection of column A and row 15.

Alpha Short for alphabetic or alphanumeric. Letters of the alphabet and numerals not classified as numeric data are treated differently from numbers by spreadsheet programs. Alpha entries are also called text entries or labels. See label, entry, concatenation.

Arithmetic operator A symbol used in spreadsheet formula entries representing a particular arithmetic operation, such as *, /, +, −, and ^ (or E) for multiplication, division, addition, subtraction, and exponentiation. See precedence.

Asynchronous scrolling Scrolling the data displayed in one screen window independently from the data displayed in another.

Blank To erase the contents from a cell or a group of cells.

Block A section of the spreadsheet containing one or more contiguous cells. The block is usually defined by specifying a range of cells. For example, the range expression A1:B2 defines the rectangular block containing cells A1, A2, B1, and B2. See address.

Block move To move the contents of one block to another block in a single operation.

Built-in A function or capability provided as an integral part of a program. See preprogrammed function.

Cell A spreadsheet location defined by the intersection of a row and a column. The column width (in characters) determines the width of the cell.

Cell contents An ambiguous expression that may refer either to the cell entry or to the displayed value.

Cell format The width of a cell; also, the manner in which the contents of a cell are displayed. A numeric cell entry, for example, may be displayed in dollars-and-cents format, exponential format, etc.

Cell locking A method for preventing a cell entry from being accidentally erased or changed.

Cell name In advanced spreadsheet programs, an arbitrary name used as a cell reference in formulas. The cell name (also called the cell designator) plays the role of a variable.

Cell reference In a formula entry, a cell address used as a variable to represent the current value in that cell.

Clear To erase the entire contents of the spreadsheet report currently loaded into the workspace.

Column A vertical division of the spreadsheet. See coordinates.

Command line The screen area where a command entered from the keyboard is displayed. Typically, a prompting message and/or a list of command options will be displayed on the command line.

Command mode The computer's state of readiness to accept and initiate a command. Also called command alert. In most spreadsheet programs, command mode is entered by pressing the slash key. See slash command.

Comment An explanatory remark or reminder inserted into the spreadsheet report at a given row or cell. In some programs, the comment is displayed on the command line but not in the cell.

Concatenation A combination of text and numeric entries within a single cell. Programs that allow concatenation are said to have "mixed cells."

Concurrent windows Same as synchronous scrolling. See scrolling.

Conditional An expression using the Boolean operator "if...then" to make one operation dependent upon the result of another.

Consolidation Combining information from two spreadsheet reports having a similar format into a single spreadsheet.

Coordinates The system of rows and columns used to identify cell locations on the spreadsheet. The column coordinates (letters of the alphabet) are normally displayed at the top of the screen and the row coordinates (numbers) along the left side of the screen. See address, hardcopy.

Copy To reproduce values or formulae from one area of a spreadsheet in another area of the spreadsheet. Some spreadsheet programs have both a copy command for one-to-one reproduction and a replicate command for one-to-many reproduction. Others use a single command, such as repeat, with options covering different types of reproduction.

Current cell See active cell.

Data Generally, any piece of information. Spreadsheet data is the information found in the cells of the spreadsheet, such as a list of expenditures for a given month, etc.

Data management function In a spreadsheet program, a function that aids in locating or manipulating spreadsheet data. Simple data management functions, such as the Lookup function, allow retrieval of an item from an indexed row or column of the spreadsheet. See preprogrammed function.

Displayed value The actual text or number displayed in a cell. The displayed value is the result of a text or numeric entry (e.g., a formula) and a specified cell format. For example, a formula entry of 100/3 may result in a displayed value of 33.33 in two-decimal format, 33 in integer format, and $33.33 in dollars-and-cents format.

Edit To correct or modify the current cell entry.

Edit/entry cursor A small cursor located on the edit line that indicates the position of the next character to be entered or edited.

Edit mode The spreadsheet program's state of readiness to accept or modify an entry. Also called edit/entry mode, entry mode, or entry alert.

Edit line A line on the screen set aside for editing or making entries. Usually the same as the prompt line.

Enter To make a spreadsheet entry from the keyboard by typing a desired label, number, or formula. Also to activate a command option by responding appropriately to a prompt message.

Entry Generally, any command issued to the program. A spreadsheet entry is the value placed in a given cell. In a strict sense, however, it is the label, number, or formula that determines what is displayed in the cell. The entry is typed on the edit line when the cell is active (when the cursor is located in the cell), and is usually completed by pressing the carriage return or Enter key. See displayed value, active cell.

Entry mode See edit mode.

First-generation spreadsheet Early spreadsheet programs, developed since 1979, such as VisiCalc, SuperCalc, and CalcStar, having limited formatting and editing capabilities.

Fixed title A title on the spreadsheet that remains fixed in place on the screen during scrolling.

Form A standardized pattern for entry and use of data. See model, template.

Format See cell format.

Forms mode A condition of the spreadsheet, specified within the template, that restricts the movement of the cursor to specific cells. Forms mode can simplify the entry of data into a standardized template (i.e., an invoice or other business form).

Formula entry A cell entry consisting of a mathematical formula. The result of the formula is displayed in the corresponding cell. In addition to the usual mathematical operators, spreadsheet formulae may use cell references as variables. For example, the formula (A1$B3) has as its result the sum of the current values located in cells A1 and B3.

Function A mathematical operation provided by the spreadsheet program to simplify formula entries. For example, the function SUM(x,y,z) results in the sum of x, y, and z. The number and complexity of functions varies from program to program, but usually includes the standard trigonometric functions, square root, etc. See preprogrammed function.

Global command A command that affects the entire contents of the spreadsheet. For example, a global formatting command will change the format of all the cells.

Goto command A command that moves the cursor immediately to any designated cell in the spreadsheet.

Graphics Pictorial display of information (e.g., a bar chart or pie chart). In particular, the use of computer graphics to produce vivid, informative pictorials.

Hardcopy A printed copy of a spreadsheet report, either in part or in its entirety. Some spreadsheet programs also provide an option to omit screen coordinates in the printed report.

Integrated spreadsheets The most powerful second-generation spreadsheets programs, with such combined functions as graphics, data management, data communications, and word processing.

Label A text entry as contrasted with a numeric entry. See concatenation.

Linking See second-generation spreadsheets.

Matrix In general, any grid of locations that will accept data; in particular, a spreadsheet template.

Mixed cell See concatenation.

Model A spreadsheet report that represents the results of possible or projected conditions; also, a template used for modeling.

Modeling Developing a spreadsheet report that projects the results of possible (What If...?) situations. In particular, creating financial projections with a spreadsheet program by changing relevant data and letting the program recalculate the financial picture based on the new entries.

Nesting The ability of an operation to include another operation of the same sort within itself. The expression "level of nesting" refers to the number of included operations.

Numeric entry An entry that displays a number as its result rather than text.

Overlay A method for transferring data from one spreadsheet directly to another spreadsheet.

Pagination Automatic division of the spreadsheet report into numbered page-sized sections so that the report may be printed out in pages.

Precedence The order in which a program processes operators in a formula. The standard order performs multiplication and division before addition and subtraction, and arithmetic operators take precedence over relational operators.

Preprogrammed function An operation that has been built into the spreadsheet program to simplify formulae. Depending upon the program, preprogrammed functions may include such operations as: the calculation of absolute value, average, day of week, duration, integer value, maximum value in a list, minimum value in a list, random selection of a value, standard deviation, sum of squares, and others. See data management function.

Print commands Command options allowing control of program output to the printer. Print command options may include printing specific areas of the spreadsheet, printing without row and column numbers, and so on.

Programmable spreadsheet A spreadsheet program incorporating a simplified programming language. This feature allows the user to create instructions that will perform sequences of operations, such as a complex group of calculations, automatically.

Protection See cell locking.

Range A continuous group of cells, defined by the addresses of the first and last cell. Usually the cell addresses that identify the range are separated by a punctuation mark (e.g., a colon or period). See block.

Recalculation Adjustment of the current spreadsheet cell values to reflect the addition to new data or a change in data. Recalculation may take place automatically after each entry, or may be suspended until a desired number of entries has been made.

Replicate See copy.

Report A spreadsheet report is made up of data entries organized within a particular template; also used to refer to the hardcopy or printout of the spreadsheet report. See template.

Row A horizontal division of the spreadsheet. See coordinates.

Save To record a spreadsheet template or report electronically, usually as a file on magnetic disk.

Screen display The portion of the spreadsheet visible on the screen, plus the status line, prompt line, command line, or edit line. See scrolling, split screen, fixed title.

Scrolling To change the screen display so that it shows a portion of the spreadsheet not currently visible. Scrolling may be done by line, screen, page, or even the entire worksheet.

Search An automatic function for locating a selected entry on the spreadsheet by carrying out a systematic search. The search function may include a replacement feature for automatic editing or deletion of one or more occurrences of the search target. Also called the find function.

Second-generation spreadsheets Spreadsheet packages with more powerful features than first-generation spreadsheets. Second-generation capabilities include building larger models, linking individual spreadsheets to form a combined report, enhanced formatting, context-sensitive help screens, additional mathematical and data management functions, text processing, and more sophisticated graphics. See integrated spreadsheets.

Security See cell locking.

Slash command A command that must be initiated by typing a preceding slash symbol, for example, the save command "/S." Many spreadsheet programs initiate command mode by means of the slash, so that the main body of spreadsheet commands are slash commands.

Sorting Alphabetic or numeric rearrangement of spreadsheet data located in a column or row. A sorting operation may provide a choice of sorting in ascending or descending order.

Spillover The ability of a spreadsheet program to accommodate a long entry by running it into adjacent cells.

Split screen A screen display that shows separate portions of the worksheet at one time by dividing the screen into two or more display areas. The individual display areas are called windows.

Spreadsheet The term spreadsheet is a general term used in many different ways; in broadest terms, a report that organizes quantities. Within a computer environment, and in this book, a spreadsheet is defined as an electronic version of an accountant's worksheet.

Spreadsheet file A file containing a spreadsheet report.

Status line A line of information, usually at the top or bottom of the spreadsheet screen, that reports the current status of the spreadsheet. The status line may display such items as the location and width of the active cell, the active cell entry, the amount of remaining memory, the dimensions of the current template, and so on.

Target The aim of a search operation or of a particular calculation.

Template The pattern of labels and formulae, located in the cells of a spreadsheet, that structure a spreadsheet report in a specific manner when data is entered. Also called a calculation format or a matrix. A template can be a simple set of labels (e.g., a list of months and days for a monthly expenditure report), or a sophisticated financial modeling template prepared by professionals and sold commercially as an add-on spreadsheet program. See spreadsheet, modeling.

Virtual memory A method for extending the amount of memory available for a spreadsheet report by utilizing disk storage space in addition to internal memory.

Window See split screen.

Worksheet In general, an accountant's columnar pad, used for recording financial data and projecting financial possibilities. In some texts, worksheet and spreadsheet are practically synonymous; in this book, the term report is generally used in place of worksheet. See report.

Appendix A

Evaluation and Review Criteria

This appendix contains a software evaluation instrument, originally designed by the Publications Division of ONE POINT (2835 Mitchell Drive, Walnut Creek, CA 94598), an independent organization that provides a variety of services and information regarding microcomputer products.

All of the spreadsheet software products reviewed in this book were evaluated by business professionals using the criterion found in this instrument. The questions concern both objective and subjective information about the program to be reviewed. A space for additional comments also is provided at the end of the booklet.

Contents

1. General Product Information
2. System & Hardware Configurations
3. Data Exchange & Program Compatibility
4. Data Integrity & Error Recovery
5. File Handling
6. Spreadsheet & Input/Edit Formatting
7. Formula Features
8. Recalculation
9. Reporting & Printing
10. Graphics Capabilities
11. Special Features
12. Documentation
13. Ease of Learning & Ease of Use
14. Support, Service & Maintenance
15. Performance & Speed
16. Program Synopsis

Copyright © 1985 by ONE POINT

General Product Information

Product Name:

Publisher:

Address:

Telephone:

List Price: $

Classification of Program:
- ☐ Spreadsheet (Stand-alone)
- ☐ Spreadsheet (Integrated package)
- ☐ Spreadsheet Template
- ☐ Spreadsheet Utility

Evaluator's System Configuration:

Evaluator:

Machine used:

Operating system:

Language written in:

Memory (K):

Number of disk drives:

Circuit cards:

Peripherals:

System & Hardware Requirements

1. Machines supported:

2. Operating systems supported:

3. Minimum memory required (K):
   Recommended (K):

4. Add-on circuit boards required:

5. Printers supported:

6. Plotters supported:

7. Monitors supported:

8. Other peripherals supported:
   ☐ Light Pen   ☐ Mouse   ☐ Other

9. Does program support multiple users?
   If yes, how many may access system?

10. Is program hard disk compatible?

11. Does program have virtual memory?

Data Exchange & Program Compatibility

1. Does the program read:
   - ☐ DIF files   ☐ ASCII files
   - ☐ SDI files   ☐ SYLK files
   - ☐ Communications
   - ☐ Other
   List programs:

2. Is the program part of an integrated
   package that includes:
   - ☐ Database management
   - ☐ File management
   - ☐ Business graphics
   - ☐ Word processing
   - ☐ Communications
   - ☐ Other
   List programs:

3. List program-compatible templates:

4. List program-compatible utilities:

Data Integrity & Error Recovery

1. Does the software allow recovery
   from a system failure, accidental reset,
   or power trouble?

2. Is a transaction (audit) file created to
   show changes since the last backup?

3. Does program have date log for file
   updating?

4. Does system automatically make
   backup files?

5. Can you locate last completed
   worksheet in the event of a power
   interruption? If yes, explain how
   (e.g., by dated disk file, etc.).

6. Does system use online error messages?

7. If the program is multiuser com-
   patible, does it provide for:
   - ☐ Worksheet lockout
   - ☐ File lockout
   - ☐ Password or access code
   - ☐ Model or operator restrictions

File Handling

1. Files displayed and selected from:
   - ☐ Menu   ☐ Screen

2. Within the program, can you:
   - ☐ Delete files   ☐ Copy files
   - ☐ Rename files
   Are these commands listed as options
   on a menu?

3. What is the max. no. of worksheets
   per file? _____

4. Can you specify that only a portion
   (range) of a model be:
   - ☐ Loaded   ☐ Saved   ☐ Printed

5. Does this program offer data channels
   linkage (several models linked together
   without having to merge entire
   models)?
   If yes, how many channels (models)
   can be linked? _____

6. Is worksheet consolidation from:
   ☐ Same file   ☐ Different files

7. Does program have single-cell linkage?
   If yes, how many links can be
   established? _____

8. Can other programs interface directly
   with the spreadsheet to read/write data?
   If not, are conversion utilities provided
   to do this?
   If yes, list the utilities:
   How would you rate the ease of use of
   the conversion program:
   ☐ Very easy   ☐ Difficult
   ☐ Easy   ☐ Impossible
   ☐ Fair

9. Can a created worksheet be joined or
   compared to existing worksheets?

Spreadsheet & Input/Edit Formatting

1. Per worksheet, what is max. no. of:
   Entries _____   Columns _____
   Rows _____   Pages _____
                         (3-D worksheet)

2. Is the column width:
   ☐ Fixed (limit) _____
   ☐ User-defined (limit) _____

   Can each column be set to unique width?
   Can you use cursor keys to set width?

3. Can blocks of cells be established
   within the spreadsheet?

4. Is there a protected entry feature for:
   ☐ Cells   ☐ Rows
   ☐ Columns   ☐ Blocks

5. Will titles of text "spill over" columns
   to complete headings?

6. Can titles be centered automatically:
   ☐ Vertically   ☐ Horizontally

7. Does program have title locking for:
   ☐ Rows   ☐ Columns

8. Does the program allow English entry
   (giving a formula or no. value a text
   or English name)?
   If yes, may text labels be integrated
   into formulae?

9. Will program allow display of formulae?

10. Can program print formulae as
    displayed?

11. Does the program page scroll:
    ☐ Vertically   ☐ Horizontally
    Is there a command to allow you to
    jump (Goto) a specific cell?
    May the arrow keys be used to move
    the cursor left, right, up, and down?

12. Within a cell, text can be:
    ☐ Right justified   ☐ Left justified
    ☐ Centered
    Numbers can be:
    ☐ Right justified   ☐ Left justified
    ☐ Centered

13. Can automatic formatting be set using:
    ☐ Dollar signs
    ☐ Automatic commas
    ☐ Decimal alignment
    ☐ Negative numbers displayed
       with parentheses

14. Does the program have a global
    search-and-replace feature?
    If yes, can you also insert non-global
    rows or columns?

15. Order in which cells can be sorted:
    ☐ Ascending   ☐ Descending
    ☐ Alphabetic   ☐ Numeric
    Are second order sorts possible?

16. Can a block be sorted?

17. Is decimal centering included?

18. Can tables be displayed across cell
    boundaries (i.e., constructing lookup
    tables in another portion of the model
    or in a separate model)?

19. Does the program offer multiple
    windows for:
    ☐ Viewing portions of one model
    ☐ Viewing portions of different
       models simultaneously
    ☐ Editing portions of one model
    ☐ Editing portions of different
       models simultaneously
    Number of windows: _____

20. Can spreadsheet structure be redefined
    online without rebuilding the data?

21. Is there a copy function?
    If yes, at what level does the copy
    function perform:
    ☐ Row   ☐ Column
    ☐ Blocks of worksheet to another
       position on the model
    ☐ An entire screen to another
       position on the model

22. Is there a copy value that converts for-
    mulae in the same range into numeric
    values in the target range?

23. Is there a replicate function?
    Does it replicate:
    ☐ By row   ☐ By column
    ☐ By blocks of a worksheet to
       another position on the model
    ☐ By an entire screen to another
       position on the model

Can you replicate:
- ☐ Formulae only ☐ Results only
- ☐ Cell format only

24. Does the program have a "lookup data" function (e.g., from a tax table)? If yes, is it:
- ☐ Horizontal ☐ Vertical
- ☐ For numbers ☐ For text

25. Can a color monitor be used with the program?
Can you select:
- ☐ Foreground color
- ☐ Background color
- ☐ Color highlights?

26. Is there a status line that displays:
- ☐ Name of model being edited
- ☐ Cursor location cell
- ☐ Width of occupied cell
- ☐ Last cell edited
- ☐ Direction of cursor when pressing Enter key
- ☐ Memory available
- ☐ Disk space available
- ☐ Other (specify):

27. Does the program allow you to specify a 40-column screen display?

Formula Features

1. Check all functions the program supports in its formulae:
Arithmetic/trigonometric/statistical functions:
- ☐ Addition ☐ Subtraction
- ☐ Multiplication ☐ Division
- ☐ Square root ☐ Sum
- ☐ Pi ☐ Raise to a power
- ☐ Integer value ☐ Absolute value
- ☐ Rounded value ☐ Tangent
- ☐ Sine ☐ Cosine
- ☐ Arc sine ☐ Arc cosine
- ☐ Arc tangent ☐ Logarithm value
- ☐ Maximum ☐ Minimum
- ☐ Average ☐ St'd deviation
- ☐ Growth by % ☐ Regression anal.

Logical/Boolean operations:
- ☐ If...Then...Else ☐ Not
- ☐ Or ☐ And
- ☐ True ☐ False

Additional features:
- ☐ Strings ☐ Searches
- ☐ String manipulation
- ☐ Local variables ☐ Global variables
- ☐ Subroutines ☐ Others (specify):

2. Can numbers be:
- ☐ An integer ☐ Decimal format
- ☐ In scientific notation

3. Numbers allowed to what digit accuracy:

Recalculation

1. Is there an automatic recalculation feature?
If yes, is it a toggle switch between auto and manual recalculation?

2. Can recalculation be performed:
- ☐ By column ☐ By row

3. Can the direction of recalculation be controlled:
- ☐ Top to bottom ☐ Left to right
- ☐ Bottom to top ☐ Right to left
- ☐ Other (specify):

Reporting & Printing

1. Can the program print the screen contents at any time?

2. Can program print in other fonts ☐
☐ other character sets ☐ in italics

3. Is there a report generator?
If yes, does the output go to:
- ☐ Screen ☐ Printer
- ☐ File

If not, is there a printing method where you can specify such output formatting as:
- ☐ Title ☐ Column headings
- ☐ Margins ☐ Column widths
- ☐ Vertical pagination
- ☐ Horizontal pagination
- ☐ Other (specify):

4. Does the spreadsheet require and support an external text editor or word processor in order to edit the format of a report?

5. Does the program provide layouts for commonly used reports?
If yes, list:

6. Can the report present data in a different order than the main file?

7. Can report forms and data layouts be saved for later use?

8. Does the report generator support special printing effects?
If yes, list:

9. Can the report generator gather data from different files?

10. Can you select reports using full Boolean operators?

11. Can you select reports based on values in the spreadsheet?

12. Can the report generator accept user-defined control/escape sequences?

13. Does the report generator have color options?

14. How would you rate the ease of use in creating reports with this spreadsheet:
    ☐ Very easy   ☐ Difficult
    ☐ Easy   ☐ Very difficult
    ☐ Fair

15. Is there a direct interface with a word processor or text editor?
    If yes, how would you rate the ease of use in creating reports with this method:
    ☐ Very easy   ☐ Difficult
    ☐ Easy   ☐ Very difficult
    ☐ Fair

Graphics Capabilities

1. Is there a graphics output capacity from:
    ☐ Program itself   ☐ Report generator
    ☐ Stand-alone business graphics package
    Specify the type of graphics produced:
    ☐ Line charts   ☐ Bar graphs
    ☐ Pie charts   ☐ Other (specify):
    Name the stand-alone business graphics program(s):

2. Does program allow for color display?

3. Per graph, how many data points will the program plot? _____
    ☐ line plots   ☐ bar plots

4. Does program make optimal use of printers or plotters w/color capabilities?

5. Can you preview the chart online before it is sent to the printer/plotter?

Special Features

1. What are the special features of program compared to similar programs?
2. Does program support macro programming?
    If yes, list special features:
    Are the macros oriented toward programmers or non-programmers?
3. Does the program come with any of the features listed below:
    ☐ Net present value
    ☐ Learning curves
    ☐ Internal rate of return
    ☐ Amortization   ☐ Future value
    ☐ Depreciation   ☐ Tax tables
    ☐ Ratios/ratio analysis
    ☐ Trend analysis   ☐ Other (specify):
4. Are there preset financial statements?

5. Are there preset budget worksheets?

6. How would you rate ease of use in creating worksheets with spreadsheet:
    ☐ Very easy   ☐ Difficult
    ☐ Easy   ☐ Very difficult
    ☐ Fair

Documentation

1. Operations manual includes:
    ☐ Index   ☐ Tabs
    ☐ Reference card   ☐ Table of contents
    ☐ Glossary of terms ☐ Registration card
    ☐ Glossary of error messages

2. Binding:
    ☐ Spiral   ☐ Hardcover
    ☐ Looseleaf   ☐ Slip case

3. Print:
    ☐ Typeset   ☐ Dot matrix
    ☐ Photocopied   ☐ Other (specify):

4. The manual includes sample exercises:

5. The manual artwork reflects:
    ☐ Menus   ☐ Printed output
    ☐ Other screen displays

6. Date of publication _____
    Last revision _____

7. How do you rate documentation as an aid for initial setup and installation:
    ☐ Excellent   ☐ Below average
    ☐ Good   ☐ Poor
    ☐ Average   ☐ None available

8. How do you rate the documentation as a user reference tool:
    ☐ Excellent   ☐ Below average
    ☐ Good   ☐ Poor
    ☐ Average   ☐ None available

9. How do you rate the clarity of the documentation:
    ☐ Excellent   ☐ Below average
    ☐ Good   ☐ Poor
    ☐ Average   ☐ None available

10. How do you rate the organization of the documentation:
    ☐ Excellent   ☐ Below average
    ☐ Good   ☐ Poor
    ☐ Average   ☐ None available

11. Program includes an online interactive tutorial?
    Tutorial can be accessed at any time?
    Rating of tutorial:
    ☐ Excellent   ☐ Below average
    ☐ Good   ☐ Poor
    ☐ Average   ☐ None available

12. Disk w/sample applications provided?
    If yes, how many?   What type?

13. Explanations/examples of program functions/commands are adequate for the average user?

14. Package includes demo disk?

15. Comments:

Ease of Learning & Ease of Use

1. Installation procedures provided for:
   - ☐ Specific microcomputer systems
   - ☐ Specific peripherals
     (e.g., printers & plotters)

   Rating of installation:
   - ☐ Very easy   ☐ Difficult
   - ☐ Easy   ☐ Very difficult
   - ☐ Fair

2. Does the program include an online interactive tutorial?
   If yes, how do you rate the tutorial's ease of use:
   - ☐ Very easy   ☐ Difficult
   - ☐ Easy   ☐ Very difficult
   - ☐ Fair

3. Does the program include sample applications on disk?
   If yes, how many?   What type?

4. Are you aware of any training aids available to the user in addition to those provided by the program itself:
   - ☐ Books   ☐ Training software

   List titles:

5. Estimated time to learn the basic functions confidently:
   - ☐ Less than 1 day ☐ 1 to 6 days
   - ☐ 1 to 2 weeks   ☐ 3 to 4 weeks
   - ☐ Over 4 weeks   ☐ Still learning

6. Are error messages provided on screen?

7. Does the package have a facility for incorporating menu sequences for automatic run mode?

8. Does the package accommodate all levels of user ability including one button access and short cuts for the experienced user?

9. Does the program make use of the function keys?

10. What would you expect to be the most difficult aspect(s) of this program for the majority of new users?
    The easiest?

11. How do you rate the overall ease of use of this program:
    - ☐ Very easy   ☐ Difficult
    - ☐ Easy   ☐ Very difficult
    - ☐ Fair

12. How experienced with personal computers should a person be in order to own this product:
    - ☐ Very exp'd   ☐ Somewhat exp'd
    - ☐ Little experience ☐ No experience

Support, Service & Maintenance

1. Provided by:

2. ☐ 800 no. ☐ Collect call ☐ Toll call

3. Days & hours support available:

4. Support terms:

5. Is the software available for evaluation purposes?

6. Copy protected?
   If yes, can program copy to hard disk?

7. Vendor backups available?

8. User must make backup copies?

9. Vendor updates available for $ _____
   Free ☐

10. Defective product replacement policy:

11. Update policy:

12. If you have tried to obtain assistance from the vendor, how do you rate that assistance:
    - ☐ Very helpful   ☐ Somewhat helpful
    - ☐ Not helpful
    - ☐ Vendor support not offered

Performance & Speed

1. Does the spreadsheet operate quickly?

2. Rate the program speed of operation during a function like recalculation, replication, or deleting/inserting rows:
   - ☐ Very fast   ☐ Slow
   - ☐ Fast   ☐ Very slow
   - ☐ Average

3. Does the program operate quickly in a multiuser environment?

4. Rate the program speed of operation during a function like recalculation, replication, or deleting/inserting rows in a multiuser environment:
   - ☐ Very fast   ☐ Slow
   - ☐ Fast   ☐ Very slow
   - ☐ Average

5. Can worksheets of one file access related worksheets of anotherfile directly?

6. Rate the frequency of disk access during operation:
   - ☐ Never   ☐ Infrequently
   - ☐ Frequently

7. Would you recommend program for its performance and speed of operation? If no, is the speed of the program hindered by:
   ☐ Hardware
   ☐ Software (i.e., language program written in)

Synopsis of the Program

1. How do you rate the overall value of this product for the price:
   ☐ Excellent value ☐ Good value
   ☐ Fair value   ☐ Poor value

2. How do you rate the overall performance of this product:
   ☐ Excellent   ☐ Below average
   ☐ Good   ☐ Poor
   ☐ Average

3. Are you satisfied with this product?

4. List the program's strengths.

5. Indicate the program's weaknesses.

6. In your opinion, what changes to the program would correct its weaknesses:

7. Additional comments:

Appendix B

Spreadsheet Software Directory

This directory contains a number of spreadsheet software products currently on the market. All software packages are listed alphabetically by product name and are available in versions that will run on the IBM Personal Computer or on IBM PC-compatible computers.

The first group of products contains all of the spreadsheet software programs reviewed in this book. Each listing includes the software publisher's name, mailing address, and telephone number.

Aura
BPI Systems, Inc.
3423 Guadalup
Austin, TX 78731
512/454-2801

Framework
Ashton-Tate
10150 W. Jefferson Blvd.
Culver City, CA 90230
213/204-5570

InteCalc
Shuchardt Software Systems
515 Northgate Dr.
San Rafael, CA 94903
415/492-9330

Multiplan
Microsoft Corp.
10700 Northup Way
Bellevue, WA 98004
206/828-8088

1-2-3
Lotus Development Corp.
161 First St.
Cambridge, MA 02142
617/492-7171

Open Access
Software Products Intl.
13043 Roselle St.
San Diego, CA 92121
619/450-1526

Report Manager
Datamension Corp.
615 Academy Dr.
Northbrook, IL 60062
312/564-5060

SuperCalc 2
SuperCalc 3
Sorcim/IUS
2195 Fortune Dr.
San Jose, CA 94131
408/942-1727

Symphony
Lotus Development Corp.
161 First St.
Cambridge MA 02142
617/492-7171

VisiCalc Package
Software Arts, Inc.
27 Mica Ln.
Wellesley, MA 02181
617/237-4000

The remaining group of spreadsheet software products contains additional tools that may be of interest to computer users. Since the products listed in this part of the directory were not reviewed or evaluated for this book, readers are advised to research these programs carefully before making a buying decision. In some cases, software vendors provide or sell demonstration disks of their programs; for further information, contact them directly.

BOS/Planner
BOS National, Inc.
2560 Royal Lane
Dallas, TX 75229
214/484-2717

CalcIT
IT Software
P.O. Box 2392
Princeton, NJ 08540
800/222-0592

CalcStar
MicroPro Intl. Corp.
33 San Pablo Ave.
San Rafael, CA 94903
415/499-1200

C-Calc
DSD
10420 NE 37th Circle −8D
Kirkland, WA 98033
206/822-2252

Context MBA
Corporate MBA
Context Management Systems
23868 Hawthorne Blvd.
Torrance, CA 90505
213/378-8277

Cope
Antech, Inc.
788 Myrtle St.
Rosewell, GA 30075
404/933-7270

Eagle Calc UNICalc
Lattice, Inc.
P.O. Box 3072
Glen Ellyn, IL 60138
312/843-2405

Easycalc
Norell Data Systems Corp.
3400 Wilshire Blvd.
P.O. Box 70127Los Angeles, CA 90010
818/502-1103

EasyPlanner
Sorcim/IUS
2195 Fortune Dr.
San Jose, CA 95131
408/942-1727

Electronic Spreadsheet
American Planning Corp.
4600 Duke St., −425
Alexandria, VA 22304
703/751-2574

Encore
Ferox Microsystems, Inc.
1701 N. Fort Myer Dr.
Arlington, VA 22209
703/841-0800

Graphplan
Chang Labs
5300 Stevens Creek Blvd.
San Jose, CA 95129
408/246-8020

Magic Worksheet
Structured Systems Group
508 Second St.
Oakland, CA 94607
415/547-1567

Micro DSS/F
Addison-Wesley Publishing Co.
Jacob Way
Reading, MA 01867
617/944-3700

MicroFCS EPS, Inc.
Evaluation & Planning Systems
One Industrial Dr.
Windham, NH 03087
603/898-1800

Microplan
Chang Labs
5300 Stevens Creek Blvd.
San Jose, CA 95129
408/246-8020

Microprophit
Via Computer, Inc.
7177 Construction Ct.
San Diego, CA 92121
800/633-1833; 800/543-4463
619/578-5356

Mycalc
Software Toolworks
15233 Ventura Blvd., –1118
Sherman Oaks, CA 91403
818/986-4885

Novacalc
Hourglass Systems
P.O. Box 312
Glen Ellyn, IL 60137
312/690-1855

Number Cruncher III
Pyramid Data
P.O. Box 10116
Santa Ana, CA 92711
714/639-1527

Peachcalc
Peachtree Software, Inc.
3445 Peachtree Rd. NE
Atlanta, GA 30326
800/554-8900; 404/239-3000

Perfect Calc
Thorne EMI Computer Software
3187C Airway Ave.
Costa Mesa, CA 92626
714/751-3778

Plan 80
Business Planning Systems
Two N State St.
Dover, DE 19901
302/674-5500

The Planner
Hayden Software, Inc.
600 Suffolk St.
Lowell, MA 01853
800/343-1218

PlanStar
MicroPro Intl. Corp.
33 San Pablo Ave.
San Rafael, CA 94903
415/499-1200

Scratchpad
Supersoft
P.O. Box 1628
Champaign, IL 61820
217/359-2112

Spread
Lupfer and Long, Inc.
P.O. Box A-57
Hanover, NH 03755
603/643-4503

Target Financial Modeling
Target Software, Inc.
1935 Cliff Valley Way, –200
Atlanta, GA 30329
404/634-9535

The Thinker
Texasoft
One Energy Square, –660
Dallas, TX 75206
214/369-0795

Timberline Spreadsheet
Timberline Systems, Inc.
7180 SW Fir Loop
Portland, OR 97223
503/684-3660

T/Maker III
T/Maker Co.
2115 Landing Dr.
Mountain View, CA 94043
415/962-0195

TMP/calc
United Software Co.
9726 E. 42nd St.
Tulsa, OK 74145
918/622-4800

UCC/MBA
University Computing Co.
UCC Tower
Exchange Park
Dallas, TX 75235
214/353-7100

UNICALC PC
Lifeboat Associates
1651 Third Ave.
New York, NY 10028
212/860-0300

**Venture Financial Planning
& Analysis System**
Weiss Associates, Inc.
127 Michael Dr.
Red Bank, NJ 07701
201/530-9260

Appendix C

Bibliography

The following references to articles, books, and other publications will provide you with further information on electronic spreadsheet software and on many of the specific products highlighted in this book.

The first section lists relevant articles from a number of well-known periodicals, most of which contain additional reviews on the software products featured in this book. For current or back issues, check local libraries and computer stores, or contact the magazine publisher directly.

The next section contains a list of books which will serve as helpful references in understanding more about using electronic spreadsheet software.

The last part of this appendix references additional publications, all of which specialize in electronic spreadsheet programs.

Periodicals

Alexander, Penny. "A Data Base within a Spreadsheet." *Business Computing,* April 1984, pp. 74-76.

Allswang, John M. "Inside Framework." *IBM PC Update,* December 1984, pp. 116-118 + .

Anderson, Dick. "A Symphonic Performance." *PC World,* July 1984, pp. 143-146.

Anderson, Dick. "Inside Symphony." *IBM PC Update,* December 1984, pp. 112-114.

Anderson, Leith. "Inside 1-2-3." *IBM PC Update,* December 1984, pp. 91-93.

Baras, Edward. "Symphony: A Community of Information." *PC Magazine,* August 7, 1984, pp. 129-135.

Bartimo, Jim. "Framework Beats the Band." *InfoWorld,* October 29, 1984, pp. 51-60.

Baxter, Ernest. "The Five-Part Symphony." *Personal Software,* July 1984, p. 60.

Berry, Timothy. "Can Spreadsheets Stand Alone?" *Business Software,* December 1984, pp. 37-40.

Berry, Timothy. "Framework Tutorial Graphing with Style." *Business Software,* December 1984, pp. 49-53.

Berry, Timothy. "Building the Big Model: Consolidating Multiple Spreadsheet Files." *Business Software,* February 1985, pp. 62-64.

Blumenthal, Stephen A. "1-2-3 Plays the Options Market." *PC World,* March 1985, pp. 212-218.

Bonner, Paul. "Symphony, a First Look." *Personal Computing,* June 1984, pp. 42-45.

Bonner, Paul. "Five Packages in One." *Personal Software,* July 1984, pp. 87-93.

Brown, Lee. "A New Aura for Integrated Software." *PC Magazine,* December 25, 1984, pp. 243-246.

Fawcette, James E. "Powerful Framework Squeezes into Conventional IBM Personal Computer." *Personal Computing,* June 1984, pp. 28-30.

Fersko-Weiss, Henry. "Avoiding Spreadsheet Disaster." *Personal Computing,* March 1985, pp. 112-117.

Flast, Robert. "Processing Your Thoughts with 1-2-3." *PC Magazine,* May 14, 1985, pp. 177-179.

Fluegelman, Andrew. "Five Complex Pieces." *PC World,* July 1984, pp. 116-125.

Foster, Edward. "Building Simple Spreadsheets." *Personal Computing,* January 1985, pp. 61-67.

Heck, Mike. "Report Manager: A Spreadsheet with a Third Dimension." *Interface Age,* June 1984, pp. 99-101.

Heck, Mike. "Aura: Four-in-One Integrated Program." *Interface Age,* October 1984, pp. 102-104.

Hogan, Thom. "From Trolls to Symphony." *Business Software,* January 1985, pp. 32-33.

Hogan, Thom. "First at the Finish Line with 1-2-3." *Business Software,* January 1985, pp. 34-37.

Hood, Ray; Goldner, Paul; and Wilding, Mike. "Do You Need the Higher-Priced Spreadsheet?" *Business Software,* January 1985, pp. 44-48.

Jadrnicek, Rik. "Review: SuperCalc3." *InfoWorld,* January 23, 1984, pp. 60-61.

Kalb, Ira. "Lotus 1-2-3 in Perspective." *Hardcopy,* May 1984, pp. 60+.

King, Richard A. "Using Multiplan in Business." *IBM PC Update,* October 1984, pp. 95-99+.

Krumm, Robert. "Comparing the Top-Selling Spreadsheets." *Business Software,* June 1984, pp. 30-38.

Layman, Don. "Framework: An Outline for Thought." *PC Magazine,* August 7, 1984, pp. 119-125.

Lipton, Russ. "Making 1-2-3 More Powerful, Less Demanding." *Business Computing,* May 1984, pp. 56-58.

McCarthy, Michael. "Spreadsheets: From A to ZZ." *Personal Software, May 1984, pp. 67+.*

McCarthy, Michael. "Getting the Most Out of Your Spreadsheet." *Personal Computing,* June 1984, pp. 136-137, 143-149.

Miller, Harry. "A Feast of Features." *PC World,* July 1984, pp. 130-138.

Miller, James. "Managing Time with SuperCalc2." *IBM PC Update,* December 1984, pp. 94-96.

Moore, William L. "VisiCalc IV: A Class Act." *Interface Age,* October 1984, pp. 100-102.

Noah, Lisa. "Hardcopy Options for 1-2-3." *Business Software,* January 1985, pp. 42-43.

Pallatto, John. "Integrated Spreadsheets." *PC Week,* June 5, 1984, pp. 35-41.

Peterson, Marty. "Review: Open Access." *InfoWorld,* April 16, 1984, pp. 46-48.

Rubin, Charles A. "Moving Up with Spreadsheet Math." *Personal Computing,* January 1985, pp. 48-57.

Scheluchin, Victor. "Open Access." *Popular Computing,* April 1985, pp. 126-130.

Sehr, Robert. "Saying It with Spreadsheets." *Personal Computing,* August 1984, pp. 79-87.

Spencer, Cheryl. "Extending the Power of 1-2-3." *Business Software,* January 1985, pp. 38-41.

Strehlo, Kevin. "A Framework for Ideas." *Personal Software,* July 1984, pp. 94-103.

Swersey, Patricia J. "SuperCalc 3." *Popular Computing,* January 1985, pp. 125-128+.

Taylor, Jared. "Thumbing Through the Spreadsheets." *PC Magazine,* April 17, 1984, pp. 144-151.

Taylor, Jared. "Advanced Report Manager Almost The Best Spreadsheet." *PC Magazine,* August 7, 1984, pp. 59-60.

Trost, Stan. "Analyzing Real Estate with 1-2-3." *IBM PC Update,* December 1984, pp. 97-101.

Walden, Jeff. "A New Formula for Spreadsheets." *Business Computer Systems,* October 1984, pp. 97-105.

Wallach, Wendell. "Lotus 1-2-3, One of the Best of the New Integrated Programs." *Small Business Computers,* Jan/Feb 1984, pp. 61 + .

Williams, David. "Spreadsheeting a Taxing Problem." *Business Software,* January 1985, pp. 49-54.

Williams, David A. "Multiplan Does Your Taxes, Part Two." *Business Software,* February 1985, pp. 57-61.

Books

Alves, Jeffrey R., and Curtin, Dennis P. *Lotus Symphony Planning and Budgeting.* New York, NY: Van Nostrand Reinhold, 1984.

Anderson, Dick. *1-2-3: Tips, Tricks, and Traps.* Indianapolis, IN: Que Corporation, 1984.

Arnold, David. *Getting Started with the IBM PC and XT.* New York, NY: Simon & Schuster, Inc., 1984.

Baras, Edward M. *Guide to Using Lotus 1-2-3.* Berkeley, CA: Osborne/McGraw-Hill, 1984.

Beil, Donald. *The VisiCalc Book.* Reston, VA: Reston Publishing Co., 1982.

Berry, Timothy. *Working Smart with Electronic Spreadsheets.* Hasbrouck Heights, NJ: Hayden Book Co., 1984.

Bolocan, David; Saechin, Kim; King, Ray; and Singer, Lauren. *Mastering Multiplan.* Blue Ridge Summit, PA: Tab Books, 1984.

Bolocan, David. *Lotus 1-2-3 Simplified.* Blue Ridge Summit, PA: Tab Books, Inc., 1984.

Cain, Thomas, and Cain, Nancy Woodward. *Lotus 1-2-3 at Work.* Reston, VA: Reston Publishing Co. 1984.

Chirlian, Barbara S. *Simply Multiplan.* Beaverton, OR: Dilithium Press, 1984.

Cobb, Douglas Ford; Cobb, Gena Berg; and Henderson, Thomas B. *Multiplan Models for Business.* Indianapolis, IN: Que Corporation, 1983.

Cobb, Douglas. *Mastering Symphony.* Berkeley, CA: Sybex, Inc., 1984.

Cobb, Douglas Ford, and Anderson, Leith. *1-2-3 for Business.* Indianapolis, IN: Que Corporation, 1984.

Cohen, Neil. *Financial Analysis with Lotus 1-2-3.* Bowie, MD: Brady Communications Co., Inc., 1984.

The Computer School. *Mastering Multiplan* Blue Ridge Summit, PA: Tab Books, Inc., 1984.

Curtin, Dennis P., and Alves, Jeffrey. *Controlling Financial Performance for Higher Profits.* New York, NY: Curtin & London, Inc., and Van Nostrand Reinhold Co., 1983.

Curtin, Dennis P., and Alves, Jeffrey. *Analyzing Your Financial Statements with Lotus Symphony.* New York, NY: Curtin & London, Inc., and Van Nostrand Reinhold Co., 1984.

Curtin, Dennis P., and Alves, Jeffrey R. *Lotus Symphony Understanding & Using Your Financial Statements.* New York, NY: Van Nostrand Reinhold, 1984.

Davis, Frederic E. *Hardware for the IBM PC and XT.* New York, NY: Simon & Schuster, Inc., 1984.

Ettlin, Walter A. *Multiplan Made Easy.* Berkeley, CA: Osborne/McGraw-Hill, 1984.

Ewing, David. *1-2-3 Macro Library.* Indianapolis, IN: Que Corporation, 1985.

Ewing, David P., and Cobb, Douglas. *The Using 1-2-3 Workbook.* Indianapolis, IN: Que Corporation, 1984.

Flast, Robert, and Flast, Lauren. *1-2-3 Run! 41 Ready-to-Use Lotus 1-2-3 Models.* Berkeley, CA: Osborne/McGraw-Hill, 1985.

Gershefski, George. *Using Lotus 1-2-3 to Solve Your Business Problems.* Totowa, NJ: Rowman & Allanheld Publishers, 1984.

Gilbert, Chris, and Williams, Laurie. *The ABC's of 1-2-3.* Berkeley, CA: Sybex, Inc., 1984.

Goodman, Danny. *How to Buy an IBM PC, XT, or PC-Compatible Computer.* New York, NY: Simon & Schuster, 1984.

Greenfield, W.M., and Curtin, Dennis P. *Cash Flow Management with Lotus 1-2-3.* Somerville, MA: Curtis & London, Inc., 1985.

Greenfield, W.M., and Curtin, Dennis P. *Cash Flow Management with Symphony.* Somerville, MA: Curtis & London, Inc., 1985.

Grushcow, Jack. *Business Worksheets for Lotus 1-2-3.* Reston, VA: Reston Publishing Co., 1984.

Harrison, William. *Framework: An Introduction.* Englewood Cliffs, NJ: Reston/Prentice-Hall, 1984.

Held, Gilbert. *IBM PC User's Reference Manual.* Hasbrouck Heights, NJ: Hayden Book Co., 1984.

Henderson, Thomas B.; Cobb, Douglas Ford; and Cobb, Gena Berg. *Spreadsheet Software from VisiCalc to 1-2-3.* Indianapolis, IN: Que Corporation, 1983.

Hergert, Douglas. *IBM PC Spreadsheets to Graphics.* Berkeley, CA: Sybex, Inc., 1984.

Hergert, Douglas. *Mastering VisiCalc.* Berkeley, CA: Sybex, Inc., 1984.

Hughes, Patricia J., and Ochi, Kaz. *Financial Analysis with Lotus 1-2-3.* Belmont, CA: Wadsworth Electronic Publishing Co., 1984.

Kelley, James E. *The IBM PC & 1-2-3.* Wayne, PA: Banbury Books, Inc., 1983.

Kenney, Donald P. *Personal Computers in Business.* New York, NY: Amacom (American Management Associates), 1985.

King, Brian L., and Philips, Sheldon W. *Framework: The Decision Maker's Guide to Business Applications.* New York, NY: Random House, 1985.

King, Richard Allen, and Trost, Stanley R. *Doing Business with Multiplan.* Berkeley, CA: Sybex, Inc., 1984.

Koff, Richard M. *Using Small Computers to Make Your Business Strategy Work.* Somerset, NJ: John Wiley & Sons, Inc., 1984.

Kruglinski, David. *Framework: The Framework Book.* Berkeley, CA: Osborne/McGraw-Hill, 1985.

LeBlond, Geoffrey T. *Using Lotus Symphony.* Indianapolis, IN: Que Corporation, 1984.

LeBlond, Geoffrey, and Cobb, Douglas. *Using 1-2-3.* Indianapolis, IN: Que Corporation, 1984.

Micro Workshop of Cambridge. *Easy as 1-2-3.* Hasbrouck Heights, NJ: Hayden Book Co., 1984.

McHugh, Kathleen, and Corchado, Veronica. *Selecting the Right Spreadsheet Software for the IBM PC.* Berkeley, CA: Sybex, Inc., 1984.

Osgood, William R., and Curtin, Dennis P. *Preparing Your Business Plan with Lotus 1-2-3.* Englewood Cliffs, NJ: Prentice-Hall, 1984.

Trost, Stanley R., *Doing Business with 1-2-3.* Berkeley, CA: Sybex, Inc., 1984.

Trost, Stanley R. *Doing Business with SuperCalc.* Berkeley, CA: Sybex, Inc., 1984.

Trost, Stanley R. *Doing Business with VisiCalc.* Berkeley, CA: Sybex, Inc., 1984.

Trost, Stanley R., and Pomernacki, Charles. *VisiCalc for Science and Engineering.* Berkeley, CA: Sybex, Inc., 1984.

Tymes, Elna, and Antoniak, Peter. *Multiplan Home and Office Companion.* Berkeley, CA: Osborne/McGraw-Hill, 1984.

Urschel, William, and Macker, Gary. *Ready to Run Accounting with Lotus 1-2-3 and Symphony.* Sherman Oaks, CA: Alfred Publishing Co., 1984.

Williams, Andrew T. *What If? A User's Guide to Spreadsheets on the IBM PC.* New York: John Wiley & Sons, Inc., 1984.

Witkin, Ruth K. *Managing Your Business with Multiplan.* Bellevue, WA: Microsoft Press, 1984.

Zimmerman, Steven; Conrad, Leo; and Zimmerman, Stanley. *Electronic Spreadsheets for the IBM PC.* Hasbrouck Heights, NJ: Hayden Book Co., 1984.

Additional Publications

Absolute Reference. Monthly journal published by the Que Corporation, 7960 Castleway Dr., Indianapolis, IN 46250. Subscriptions: $60/yearly. Designed for users of 1-2-3, each issue has information on how to get full usage from the power of 1-2-3 from Lotus Development Corporation.

SpreadSheet. Monthly newsletter published by InterCalc, P.O Box 4289, Stamford, CT 06907. Subscriptions: $42/yearly, includes membership; $7.50 an issue to non-members. This newsletter, published by the International Electronic Spreadsheet Users' Group (formerly VisiGroup), focuses on tips and gives workable examples for all spreadsheets.

Trademark Acknowledgments

The companies listed below hold trademarks (shown in italics) on the following products which are mentioned in the book.

Ashton-Tate *dBASE II, dBASE III, Framework*
BPI Systems, Inc. *Aura, BPI Accounting Series*
Datamension Corporation *Project Manager, Records Manager, Report Manager, Task Manager*
Digital Research *CP/M, CP/M-86*
Epson American, Inc. *Epson Printers*
Florida Data Corporation *Florida Data Printers*
Hercules Computer Technology *Hercules Graphics Card*
International Business Machines Corporation *IBM Personal Computer, IBM PC, PC-XT, PC-AT, PC-DOS*
ID Systems Corporation *IDS Printers*
Lotus Development Corporation *Lotus, 1-2-3, Symphony*
MicroPro International *WordStar*
Microsoft Corporation *Microsoft, Microsoft BASIC, MS-DOS, Multiplan, Symbolic Link (SYLK)*
Okidata Corporation *Okidata Printers*
Schuchardt Software Systems, Inc. *InteCalc, InteMate, IntePert, IntePlan, InteSoft Series, InteWord*
Software Arts *Data Interchange Format (DIF), VisiCalc, VisiCalc Package*
Software Products International *Open Access*
Sorcim/IUS Micro Software *SuperCalc, SuperCalc2, SuperCalc3, SuperData Interchange (SDI)*
Tandy Corporation *TRS-80 Modem II*
Trustees Dartmouth College *BASIC*

One Point is a trademark of One Point, a California corporation. The use of any additional trademarks is for reference purposes only.

Index